slices of life:

Managing Dilemmas in Middle Grades Teaching
Case Studies for Professional Development

David Mandzuk and Shelley Hasinoff

National Middle School Association
Westerville, Ohio

April Tibbles, Director of Publications
John Lounsbury, Editor, Professional Publications
Carla Weiland, Publications Editor
Cynthia Ritter, Grahic Designer
Ann Draghi, Graphic Designer
Dawn Williams, Publications Manager
Marcia Meade-Hurst, Senior Publications Representative
Derek Neal, Publications & Membership Marketing Manager

Library of Congress Cataloging-in-Publication Data

Mandzuk, David.
  Slices of life : managing dilemmas in middle grades teaching : case studies for professional development / David Mandzuk and Shelley Hasinoff.
      p. cm.
  Includes bibliographical references.
  ISBN 978-1-56090-239-3
  1. Middle school teaching--United States--Case studies. 2. Middle school teachers--Training of--United States--Case studies. 3. Middle school teachers--Professional relationships--United States--Case studies. I. Hasinoff, Shelley. II. Title.
  LB1623.5.M25 2010
  373.1102--dc22
                            2010019259

National Middle School Association
4151 Executive Parkway, Suite 300
Westerville, Ohio 43081
1-800-528-NMSA f: 614-895-4750
www.nmsa.org

Acknowledgements

We would like to acknowledge the following individuals for contributing to this collection of case studies: Sheila Alexander, Paul Anderson, Jamie Angus, Rob Bell, Trevor Borland, Angela Busch, Melissa Cerkow, Paul Connor, Anne-Marie Dooner, Jason Ducharme, Tammy Esdale, Rick Farmer, Angela Gelineau, Kevin Goetz, Valerie Hill, Jamie Hutchison, Jennifer Kasian-Machovec, Neil Klassen, Marlene Lypoudis, Buffie Macklin, Cam Steuart, Cyndi Tibbs, Melissa Ting, Jeff Warkentin, Glenna Williams, and Vanessa Young.

About the Authors

David Mandzuk, Ph.D., has been teaching in the public school system and at the post-secondary level in Winnipeg, Canada, for over 30 years. He has acted as a classroom teacher, a physical education teacher, a cooperating teacher, a faculty advisor, and a faculty associate. In 2000, he joined the Faculty of Education at the University of Manitoba as an assistant professor in middle years education, in 2003, he was appointed as Associate Dean (Undergraduate Programs), and in 2006 he became an associate professor. He has published widely in national and international journals and lives in Winnipeg, Canada, with his wife, Lynda, and his two daughters, Jayne and Andrea.

Shelley Hasinoff, Ph.D., has been teaching for over 30 years at all levels and in three Canadian provinces. She has acted as a resource teacher, a coordinator for gifted and talented students, a faculty associate in the middle years program at the University of Manitoba, a principal of a private school, and a consultant on assessment and evaluation. Along with David Mandzuk, and on her own, she has published widely in academic journals. She is currently coordinator of the Independent Education Unit for Manitoba Education and was one of the contributing writers to the provincial document "Engaging Middle Years Students in Learning: Transforming Middle Years Education in Manitoba," released in March 2010. She and her husband Brian live in Winnipeg, Canada. They have a son, Sam, and a daughter, Amy.

Contents

contents continued

Chapter 1

When There Is No Right Answer: Managing the Messiness of Teaching

Teaching is a "messy" business. Whatever you think when you begin teaching, you are never fully prepared for the many times when you are faced with real dilemmas that have no right or wrong answers. Sometimes, the best you can hope for is to be able to manage a situation with your integrity intact. This book is about those times.

Before you begin reading, we think it would be helpful if you had some idea of how this book came to be and how it has evolved. The case studies in this collection were written, in large part, by students in a faculty of education at a large midwestern university. Students were asked to identify dilemmas in their teaching and write case studies on them. Following common practice, the names and details have been significantly altered to protect the privacy of the individuals and schools involved. The purpose of the assignment was to give students the opportunity to recreate the situations that they experienced firsthand and then to reflect on those situations not only from their perspectives as student teachers, but also from the perspectives of others who may have been involved. This is one of the advantages of case studies—they can really help us see situations through the eyes of others, and of course, this skill is fundamental to effective teaching. Another purpose of the case study assignment was to respond to the age-old criticism of teacher education programs—that they are not practical enough and don't prepare student teachers for some of the realities that await them in the schools. Although this connection with practice is important, we strongly believe that teachers also need to appreciate the value of theory.

In the writing of this book, one thing we observed was that although there are many case study books on teaching, many of them lack a theoretical framework. Although the appeal of case studies is certainly their practical application, we believe that educators need to try to meld theory and practice, or they run the risk of making decisions based on intuition and rooted in the "mythology" of teaching rather than professional "knowledge" (Clifton, 1989). Considering theory when reading case studies enables educators to generalize across situations and anticipate dilemmas before they actually occur. Furthermore, when educators step back to consider perspectives other than their own, they are more likely to see the bigger picture and the longer term implications of their actions.

The approach we have used in *Slices of Life: Managing Dilemmas in Middle Grades Teaching* is to use the cases as vehicles for analysis, inquiry, and problem solving. According to Kleinfeld (1992, p. 35), when cases are used in this way, they help student teachers acquire the situated knowledge of teaching they need in order to "think like a teacher" and to acquire the habits of analysis, inquiry and reflection. Beynon, Geddis, and Onslow (2001) remind us that "educational dilemmas do not happen in neat, tidy boxes, which pertain to specific issues. Rather, teachers often find themselves entwined in a dozen quandaries at the same time."

We think that the case study approach and the application of theory contribute to our understanding of the complexities of teaching and learning and help us to manage dilemmas. Making the distinction between problematic situations that have simple solutions and those that are real dilemmas, and therefore less amenable to quick fixes (Lampert, 1985; 1986), is the first task in trying to manage dilemmas.

Who will use this book?

We envision two main audiences for *Slices of Life: Managing Dilemmas in Middle Grades Teaching*. The first audience will be teacher educators who may use it as a primary resource or as a complementary text in courses designed to prepare middle grades teachers. The second audience will be professional learning communities, particularly those in schools that serve as practicum sites. Because the book provides a framework for critically examining many common issues that arise in middle schools, we can envision middle grades teachers and administrators, teaching partners, grade level teams, and whole staff discussion groups making use of the book to examine their practices together. We hope that our approach will engage you in meaningful discussions about the relationship between theory and the realities of teaching in the middle grades and that those discussions will contribute to your ongoing professional growth.

Distinguishing between problems and dilemmas

Throughout their careers, teachers are continually faced with problems that make teaching interesting and challenging. But are all problematic situations identical? Beynon, Geddis, and Onslow (2001) along with Lampert (1985) argue that a distinction can be made between *problems* and *dilemmas* in teaching. They suggest that problems are situations that can be resolved relatively easily once a number of possible resolutions are identified. For instance, a situation involving a disagreement between two students over the ownership of a skateboard might easily be classified as a problem. One way for a teacher to resolve this problem might be to have each student in the conflict explain his/her side of the story to the other in order to sort fact from fiction. Another way might be for a teacher to call the students' parents to see if they might be able to resolve the problem at home. A third way might be for a teacher to ask other students to provide "insider information" that might get to the bottom of skateboard ownership.

And, like most teachers, we, too, have agonized over problematic situations in our teaching practice and invested a considerable amount of time and energy searching for solutions that sometimes didn't even exist.

Situations of this type are dilemmas, which are "messier" and more complex than problems, and as Beynon et al. (2001) and Lampert (1985) point out, cannot actually be resolved. Furthermore, researchers such as Katz and Raths (1992) and Room (1985) suggest that dilemmas are characterized by having: (a) at least two courses of action, each of which is problematic, and (b) one course of action that sacrifices the advantage that might have accrued if the alternative was chosen. Lampert (1985) believes that the best we can expect to do with dilemmas is to manage them. She suggests that managing dilemmas involves a series of losing arguments that we have with ourselves as we consider the merits and limitations of the various alternatives. She also argues that by managing rather than trying to resolve what are essentially irresolvable dilemmas, we are ultimately admitting some essential limitations to our control over human problems.

Types of dilemmas. Dilemmas can be *philosophical* such as the debate teachers might have over the pros and cons of integrating students with diverse learning needs. Dilemmas can also be *political* such as the dilemma a principal might face when confronted by a parent who is able to use his position of authority to influence school policy. Dilemmas can even be *pedagogical* such as the dilemma a teacher might have in deciding whether or not it is best practice to administer a government-mandated standardized test to her special needs students. Dilemmas, whether they are philosophical, political, or pedagogical, deeply challenge educators, but perhaps the most perplexing dilemmas are those that are described as moral dilemmas.

Moral dilemmas. According to Strike, Haller, and Soltis (1988), moral dilemmas have three major characteristics. First, moral dilemmas concern what is the fair or the right thing to do, not just the most expedient or least troublesome. Moral issues are usually characterized by words such as "right," "ought," "just," and "fair" and they concern our obligations to one another. Second, moral dilemmas cannot be settled by just the facts alone. Obviously, facts are important in thinking about moral questions but they are not sufficient unto themselves. Finally, beyond the facts, resolving moral dilemmas involves understanding what principles, such as fairness and equity, underlie our moral decisions. Moral dilemmas often occur when people's moral sentiments conflict; for example, a teacher who wants to show empathy towards one student but also wants her actions to be perceived as fair to the entire class.

Using theory to manage dilemmas

Once we recognize a dilemma as a dilemma, we can begin to consider possible ways of managing it in light of what we know about teaching and learning in the middle grades. To manage the dilemma, one must be clear what the principles are, how they can be justified, and which principle takes priority. Put this way, managing dilemmas seems straightforward enough, but we know from our own experiences as teachers that, in practice, the process can be messy and very challenging.

One helpful strategy for managing dilemmas is to uncover and understand the underlying tensions that give rise to them. Many of the most common dilemmas that challenge educators arise from tensions that underlie one of the following dimensions: *diversity, collegiality, identity, community*, and *authority*. In Part One we explore each of these dimensions and expose the tensions that underlie them.

- Chapter 2, *Diversity: Striving for Excellence and Equity*, explores dilemmas that arise when educators try to accommodate the needs of diverse learners while maintaining high academic standards.

- Chapter 3, *Collegiality: Balancing Autonomy and Conformity,* considers dilemmas that occur when teachers try to maintain their individuality in the face of pressures to make teaching decisions based on the consensus of the team.

- Chapter 4, *Identity: Making the Transition from Student to Teacher,* examines dilemmas that surface when educators try to accomplish the tasks of professional socialization while playing different and sometimes conflicting roles.

- Chapter 5, *Community: Understanding Social Capital,* probes dilemmas that happen as educators and parents transact personal and social relationships.

- Chapter 6, *Authority: Finding the Balance to Engage Learners,* addresses dilemmas that come about as educators try to navigate the complex terrain of social relationships and subject matter expertise.

For each dilemma we provide a theoretical overview that is followed by a realistic case study. We analyze the dilemma in the case from the perspective of the dimensions and their underlying tensions, and finally, we present three questions that we hope will lead the reader to a broader understanding of both the concept and the case. The first question focuses on the case itself, the second question helps the reader to consider the underlying tension, and the last question provides a scaffold for the reader to apply the case to their own practice.

In Part Two, we acknowledge that in the real world of teaching, the dimensions of *diversity, collegiality, identity, community,* and *authority* are not as distinct as we present them in Part One. In reality, these five dimensions are interrelated in interesting but challenging ways. For example, a case involving students who challenge the authority of their teacher may reflect the diversity of students in a class and may point to poor relationships within a school community. Similarly, a case involving a conflict between a student teacher and his cooperating teacher might involve issues of identity, authority and collegiality. We describe and model a four-step analytical process for the first case and then provide nine more cases for readers to analyze on their own using the four steps:

1. Describe the dilemma(s) in the case and specify who "owns" the dilemma(s).

2. Determine which dimensions and underlying tensions apply to the dilemma(s).

3. Identify alternatives for managing the dilemma(s) and consider what criteria you will use to evaluate these alternatives.

4. Decide which alternative is the best and explain why.

Each of the cases is followed by three questions. Like the questions in Part One, the first question addresses the case itself, the second question addresses the dimensions and their underlying tensions, and the third question asks readers to relate the case to their own experience.

We close the book with a glossary and references that are conveniently arranged by section.

The Five Dimensions of Teaching

Part One

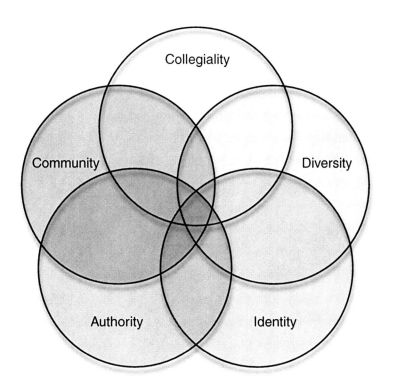

Chapter 2

Diversity: Striving for Excellence and Equity

Classrooms today are expected to be warm, inviting, and challenging environments for males and females, physically disabled and non-disabled learners, and native English speakers and those who are learning English as an additional language. Classrooms are also expected to be welcoming towards students from mainstream cultures as well as those from minority and marginalized backgrounds, students with learning disabilities, gifted and talented learners, and students with unique combinations of physical, emotional, and social needs. Managing diversity is a tall order for today's teachers. Nevertheless, it is not an option. Teachers are directed by legal, moral, and pedagogical imperatives to make every possible effort to meet the needs of every learner in every classroom.

Legal, moral, and pedagogical imperatives

"Success for All Learners" and "No Child Left Behind" are not just catchphrases, but rather signify serious expectations supported by laws. In the United States, landmark cases, such as Oberti v. Board of Education of the Borough of Clementon School District (Oberti v. Clementon, 1993) have set the standard for what schools are expected to provide, and Public Law 94-142 has long set the standard for a wide range of policies and services for educating "handicapped" students. Although the courts are moving away from mandating inclusive placements as a matter of right or law, they are increasingly ruling that students with disabilities should be educated with their non-disabled peers to the extent possible. Teachers are expected to make whatever adaptations are necessary to enable students to be academically successful. Adaptations include giving students more time, arranging for alternate settings for testing, enhancing audio or visual delivery, offering options for students to meet learning outcomes, and establishing various grouping arrangements.

In addition to legal imperatives, leading educational thinkers such as Thomas Sergiovanni, Nel Noddings, Roland Barth, and Michelle Borba argue that schools are morally obligated to create a culture of caring in which all students feel valued and have a sense of belonging. High profile events such as the tragedies at Columbine, Colorado, and Taber, Alberta, and growing concerns about the extent and seriousness of bullying (Colorosso, 2004; Olweus, 2003) have resulted in widespread campaigns to increase awareness and tolerance of individual differences. Teachers need to know their students well and demonstrate such understanding through appropriate attention to their students' needs; in other words, schools must accommodate all types of diversity as a matter of course.

Accommodating diversity is also supported by research into how the brain learns (Wolfe, 2001). Increasingly, textbooks and instructional materials reflect this research and the understanding that meaning is individually, actively, and socially constructed. Teachers are expected to adopt approaches that reflect this understanding, such as providing students with ample opportunities to discuss and reflect with others through frequent, specific, and positive feedback; involving students in developing and assessing their own and their peers' learning; and offering students a variety of ways to express themselves.

Legal, moral, and pedagogical imperatives not only direct teacher behavior but also expand our understanding of what diversity means. In the past, we used the term *diversity* to talk about a small number of students who were integrated into mainstreamed classrooms for part of their education. More recently, we have used this term to describe students in our classrooms who come from different socioeconomic backgrounds or who represent a variety of cultural, linguistic, and ethnic groups.

As Tomlinson, Moon, and Callahan (1998) point out,

> Diversity is a hallmark of middle level learners. Middle schoolers range from child-like to adult-like, from socially awkward to socially adept, from emotionally insecure to brimming with confidence, and from concrete to abstract in thinking—sometimes seemingly all in the same student on the same day (p. 3).

Whether we are referring to students with special needs, students from different backgrounds, or the developmental variation among middle grades students, Sapon-Shevin (2000) argues "We must move beyond discussions of diversity as a problem in the classroom to a conception of differences as natural, inevitable, and desirable, enriching teaching and learning experiences for teachers and students alike" (p. 35).

Philosophically, it is difficult to argue with this ideal. Nevertheless, there are very real challenges for schools who wish to create environments that not only acknowledge all of the differences among students but also support them to be socially and academically successful. Middle grades teachers wonder how they can maintain high expectations in classrooms where some students still struggle to decode simple text or to learn English as a second (or even a third) language. As refugees from war-torn countries or as members of impoverished communities, some students may be ill-equipped for learning or unsupported in their efforts to secure an education. Still others may have physical, cognitive, or social disabilities that require more attention than a single teacher can provide. Added to these challenges are the developmental concerns of middle grades students who may resist individualized attention because they do not wish to appear to be different from their peers. Parents, for their part, may also actively reject any accommodations for fear that their children may be stigmatized.

Equity and excellence

A key question in coping with this diversity is, "How can we be certain that we don't sacrifice the needs of the group as we attempt to meet the needs of individual students?" Underlying this question are two pivotal values—equity and excellence.

> Historically, the middle school movement reflects a strong equity perspective. Historically, proponents focusing largely on the educational needs of high ability learners reflect a strong excellence perspective. Some perceive these to be competing values, a "zero sum game" in contemporary parlance. To support access to opportunity for many, some would say, is to diminish emphasis on high-end quality for a few, and vice versa. (Tomlinson & George, 2004, p. 8)

The tension between excellence and equity in middle schools appears most evident in discussions about ability grouping for specific subjects, most notably in mathematics. Critics of tracking argue that it condemns low-performing students to low expectations and impoverished learning experiences that focus on remediation rather than substance. Despite strong advocacy to reduce or eliminate tracking or ability grouping in middle grades, researchers have consistently found that homogeneous grouping increases as students move through middle school, though full tracking has decreased. Interestingly, some schools unwittingly create de facto tracks by assigning options such as band, art, foreign languages, athletics, or computer skills to fixed groups that take on the qualities of academic streams. In any event, by Grade 8, students are invariably grouped by ability for at least part of their day, often in honors English or

International Baccalaureate courses for advanced students and remedial reading and differentiated math classes for struggling students.

Despite the strong support for more inclusive classrooms and marked success when practiced, heterogeneous grouping remains controversial. Parents sometimes wonder if their so-called "average" children will have less teacher time and attention and will therefore achieve less. However, the presence of students with severe disabilities has not been found to have an effect on levels of allocated or engaged time. Furthermore, there was no significant difference in the amount of time lost to interruptions of instruction between inclusive and non-inclusive classrooms. Both parents and educators have expressed concern that heterogeneous grouping may slow down the learning of high-achieving students. These concerns are somewhat supported by evidence that high achievers do better in accelerated classes for the gifted and talented (Kulik & Kulik, 1991).

However, Oakes, Selvin, Karoly, and Guiton (1992) argue that it is not homogeneous grouping that makes the difference, but rather it is the enriched curriculum that accounts for the gains made by highly able students in separate classes. Moreover, they argue that all students, particularly lower track students, thrive on an advanced curriculum given the appropriate supports.

Indeed, educators increasingly believe that segregating students by diagnosis or handicap is not in their best interests. Inclusion, now widely practiced, promotes greater acceptance of disabled students by their peers and greater gains in academic achievement. As students become more successful in regular classrooms, parental expectations increase and students become more capable of achieving.

Differentiation

We need to take a different approach because our traditional, outdated practices simply reinforce assumptions about disability. Rather than making individual students fit into our existing school programs, we need to make changes that will allow diverse students to experience greater success in our schools. To this end, many districts and schools have embraced differentiation as an effective means of meeting the diverse needs of students.

> A differentiated classroom offers a variety of learning options designed to tap into different readiness levels, interests, and learning profiles. In a differentiated class, the teacher uses: (1) a variety of ways for students to explore curriculum content, (2) a variety of sense-making activities or processes through which students can come to understand and "own" information and ideas, and (3) a variety of options through which students can demonstrate or exhibit what they have learned. (Tomlinson, 1995, p. 2)

Although differentiation may be a key strategy for dealing with diversity, research suggests that new teachers may have considerable difficulty differentiating instruction. In particular, novices were unclear about the meaning of differentiation and did not know how to translate it into classroom practice. Indeed, in an interview with Mary Ann Hess (1999), Tomlinson characterizes the problem as follows:

> Young teachers are developing the gross motor skills of teaching. Differentiation is a fine motor skill. The way to get there is to teach them to look at kids as individuals and to let kids show you what they can do…In truth, differentiation probably calls for an expert teacher.

However, Gould (2004) rejects this argument in an article entitled "Can Novice Teachers Differentiate Instruction? Yes They Can!" She argues that novice teachers can learn to differentiate their instruction when they are explicitly taught how and when teacher educators in the faculty and in the field expose them to effective modeling.

The following case illustrates the impact of diversity on a classroom teacher. As the case unfolds, a veteran teacher is forced to examine her long-held beliefs and the delicate balance required to support diverse learners and still maintain grade level standards.

The case: Questioning Inclusion

Susan Bond had been teaching at Riverview Middle School for 23 years. She led the school's transformation from a junior high to a middle school about three years ago and continued to be a respected member of the school's faculty. She was the leader of one of the school's four interdisciplinary teams and was known for her commitment to the heterogeneous grouping of students.

Susan taught social studies to her 7th grade homeroom class of 16 boys and 11 girls in the first period after lunch every other day. Two of Susan's students were funded special needs students. Mitch had been diagnosed with Asperger's Syndrome, a pervasive developmental disorder that affected his social relationships and often meant that he engaged in repetitive behaviors, while Daniel had a speech and language disorder stemming from a hearing impairment. Susan developed individual education plans for each of the boys, and these were thoughtfully implemented by Brian Black, the education assistant. Brian generally positioned himself between the two boys, maintaining their focus and ensuring that they were able to keep up, as much as possible, with what was happening in the class.

One Monday afternoon, as the students filed into the room and took their seats, it appeared that some kind of disagreement had taken place over lunch. Two of the boys, Maryk and Tim were speaking loudly and staring angrily at each other as they entered the room. Their disagreement ended when Susan asked everyone to take a seat. Maryk took his seat as requested, but he continued to glare at Tim.

Susan began the class by reminding the students that they had come to the end of the unit. "Get out your double-entry notebooks, please," she said. "Be ready if I call your name to come to the front of the class and present your group's research findings to the rest of the class." Susan reached into the "talking jar" and pulled out the names. By now, her students were comfortable with the routine and understood that each one of them was expected to be ready to present and to take detailed notes on other students' presentations. Susan got out her assessment binder with the rubric she had co-constructed with the class at the beginning of the unit. She planned to jot brief anecdotal notes in the margins of her grade book, knowing that these would be very helpful when she met with parents later that month.

Susan looked at the first name she had pulled out of the jar and called on Derek to come forward. He had no sooner started to speak when whispers between Maryk and Tim escalated into an all-out shouting match. Susan went quickly to where the boys were sitting and instructed them to step into the hallway with her. Maryk suddenly threw his books on the floor and insisted that Tim was completely to blame. As Tim put up his fists and started yelling back at Maryk, Susan realized that the boys would need extra time to cool down, and so she motioned to Brian to come and escort the boys to the office. She knew that once Maryk and Tim cooled down and Brian and the principal had a chance to help them resolve what was troubling them, that they would be able to resume their on-again, off-again friendship.

Susan sighed to herself. It was the rare Monday that the class managed to proceed without one or the other groups in the class erupting over some real or imagined slight. She understood that middle grades students could be volatile, but tempers were aggravated by tensions that existed between diverse ethnic and religious groups that made up the school community. This meant that petty squabbles between adults often spilled over into the school and some students were so completely distracted by the conflicts that they were unable to concentrate on what was going on in the class. Susan knew that Maryk and Tim were among the students most affected by what was happening in the community. Sometimes, she felt as though she was fighting a losing battle to keep her students from falling further and further behind. To make matters worse, she was unable to count on many of their parents to help because their command of English was rudimentary at best, and they were either unwilling or unable to take time from their work to meet with teachers. Children in this community were left mostly to their own devices and homework was rarely supervised. Although Susan worked hard to develop a positive classroom atmosphere based on mutual respect, it seemed that every step she took forward with them as a group meant two steps backwards, especially after the weekend.

Susan turned her attention back to the class and tried to settle them down to the task at hand. She asked Derek to carry on with his presentation and although there were no further eruptions, the rest of the students were clearly unsettled by what had just happened. As Susan cast her eyes to the back of the room, she couldn't help but notice that Mitch and Daniel were like two lost souls without Brian to guide them. They weren't taking notes, and they did not appear to be taking in much of anything else either. Susan knew that Maryk and Tim's outburst was even harder for these two to handle and she knew that as long as Brian wasn't there to calm them down and to guide their note-taking, the rest of the class would likely be a waste of time for them.

"Anything wrong, Susan?" She looked up and saw John Saunders, one of her colleagues, peeking around the corner of the doorway during the break between classes. She reviewed what had happened and then said in a hushed tone, "I am so frustrated! How can I manage inclusion when my class is so diverse? How can I meet all of my students' needs? On one hand there are Mitch and Daniel who are struggling to keep up and they have Brian to help them most of time! On the other hand, there are the students that just can't keep up with the assignments and are falling further and further behind. They get no support from their homes, and there is so little time to spend in class just catching up. I am certain that Maryk and Tim and for that matter Gus, Jason, Joy and Ali would be far more successful academically if someone could just work with their communities to reduce the tensions between them. On top of that, Brian is talking about returning to university in the fall and if he does, I don't know what I will do without his help. At this point in my career, the last thing I want to have to do is break in someone new."

"I know just what you mean, Susan," said John. "I have the same conflicts erupting in the 8th grade science class, and Theresa, my educational assistant, is run off her feet trying to help the four special needs students in my class. It's not getting any easier, that's for sure! I don't know about you, but with all the time I spend working with Theresa and those four students, I feel that I am neglecting the rest of the kids in my class. I hate to say it, but maybe we should revisit our policy of heterogeneous grouping. Let's put this on the agenda for our next team meeting and seriously consider approaching the administration for some additional support."

As Susan and John returned to their respective classes, they each wondered what they could do to alleviate the pressure they were feeling. How could they address the needs of their diverse learners without holding back the progress of the rest of their students?

Using theory to inform practice

This case highlights the dilemma that teachers face when they are trying to resolve the tension between equity and excellence. What follows is an analysis of the case from the perspective of diversity.

Susan and her colleagues recognize that diversity is characteristic of the middle grades and agree in principle that heterogeneous grouping is an important means of integrating students with a wide range of physical, emotional, cognitive, and social differences. However, they are beginning to have doubts about whether they can meet the diverse needs of the students in their classrooms, even with support from educational assistants. When their educational assistants are diverted to other tasks and when outside sources of conflict create barriers between student groups, their strategies for coping with diversity begin to break down.

Robert Putnam (2007), in a study of 30,000 people across America, exposes what Jonas (2007) calls the "downside of diversity." Putnam makes the case that while diversity is ultimately enriching, valuable, and necessary for creative responses to difficult problems, smoothing over the divisions among diverse groups requires enormous effort because in very diverse communities often people not only don't trust people of other ethnic backgrounds, they don't trust each other much either. Putnam calls for targeted support for English-language instruction and investing in community centers, athletic fields, and schools where "meaningful interaction across ethnic lines" can occur. The diversity that Susan sees in her classroom and the conflicts that can arise as a result reflect what is occurring in the wider community. She is aware that the school cannot solve the problems alone, and although she speculates that the community needs assistance, she does not seem to realize the important role that the school could play in reaching across ethnic lines.

Indeed, in Susan's classroom, it may be that the most important learning outcomes she can target have to do with learning the tools of active citizenship. She and her students could work together on constructing criteria to create a rubric about relationships with others. She needs to expand her notion of inclusion to mean the involvement of special needs students with their peers and not just with the adults in the classroom. By really examining the struggles faced by many of her students, she may determine that the most important thing she can do is not to wait for someone else to assist the community, but to make the problems of the community the content of her social studies class. She needs to find ways to open the doors of her classroom to the community and to open the community to the school. She could train her students to become community ambassadors and invite non-English speaking parents to speak to the class with their children as translators. The more opportunities she can find to create interactions that cross ethnic lines, the more likely students will learn to become more culturally competent and begin to celebrate diversity as strength.

Recent school improvement initiatives have been driven by renewed public pressure to maintain high expectations for all students and to foster excellence in schools. This pressure stems in part from unfavorable rankings in international tests and from a growing economic concern that prosperity may begin to desert Western nations as more populated parts of the world become more industrialized and conduct more of their business in English. At the same time, as we pointed out earlier in this section, schools are pressured by legal, pedagogical, and moral imperatives to create greater equity for all students in schools.

Unfortunately, for many parents and educators, excellence is all too often seen as being at odds with equity and there are many who believe that it is a "zero-sum game" (Robbins, 2007). In other words, if we have excellence we can't have equity and if we have equity we can't have excellence. However, Lupart (1999) and others argue that the opposite is true—excellence and equity cannot exist apart and equity is a pre-condition for excellence. Although many educators agree with this stance, it may seem overwhelming at times to implement it in highly diverse classrooms.

Perhaps, the perceived conflict between the excellence and equity problem lies in thinking that serving the interests of "equity" means treating everyone "the same" and expecting everyone to do the same work, albeit with assistance. Classrooms that use differentiation as a strategy have the potential of meeting the goals of both excellence and equity. Unfortunately, differentiation is often not well understood. For some teachers, differentiation just means using a variety of instructional methods with the whole class. However, this is a hit-and-miss strategy that is unlikely to result in appropriate instruction for every student in the class. In a differentiated classroom, all students are expected to meet the same outcomes but not necessarily by the same routes or on the same day. When teachers recognize that some students will need more time to work on basic concepts and others may be able to move more quickly into application activities, the focus shifts from covering content to helping each student learn.

Differentiation requires a careful planning process like that described by Wiggins and McTighe (2005) as backward design. Teachers using this method of planning begin by first identifying what outcomes are important to meet rather than thinking first about what activities to prepare or what pages in the text to assign. Once teachers decide on the outcomes, they determine which types of assessment (e.g., written, oral, or performance) will be best for showing evidence that students have met the outcomes. Finally, teachers design the activities and experiences that will scaffold learning and allow students to meet the outcomes in a variety of ways that are appropriate to their needs and abilities.

In this case, there is no evidence that Susan or John has differentiated instruction or offered different opportunities for their students, with special needs or not, to demonstrate their understanding. The culminating activity of the unit, for example, involves all students in the class demonstrating evidence of their learning in the same way. Furthermore, Susan obviously depends on her educational assistant to mediate learning for Mitch and Daniel and to help them "keep up." If Susan was using differentiated instruction and assessment, there would have been opportunities for students to make choices about how they demonstrated their learning, and the activities would be varied by type, grouping, the level of abstractness, and the difficulty level of resources. By planning differentiated instruction, Susan and her colleagues might begin to organize their teaching more effectively to deal with the diversity of their students and feel less frustrated in the attempt to meet their needs.

Think about the tension between excellence and equity in your own school. Whose needs are seen to be more important—the needs of individual students or the needs of the group? How can we meet every learner's needs? Is it even realistic to think that we can?

Case Discussion Questions

1. In your opinion, are students like Mitch and Daniel served best by being integrated into the regular classroom or by being segregated in special classes? If so, what are the challenges in doing so? What might some other options be?

2. Like Susan and John, teachers sometimes wonder how they can balance the demands for equity and excellence in their classrooms. What do you think schools can do to meet the needs of all learners?

3. Susan begins to question whether or not she is meeting her students' needs. Is it practical for her to try to reach out to a divided community? What would you do if you were in her shoes?

Chapter 3

Collegiality: Balancing Autonomy and Conformity

Teaching has long been characterized as an isolating profession, and the lack of meaningful collaboration among teachers has often been lamented. Traditionally, teachers, whether in self-contained or departmentalized situations, have taught independently with relatively little contact with their peers, even though they may have taught across the hall or next door to one another. Little (1990a) has characterized the persistent isolation of teachers in these words:

> In large numbers of schools and for long periods of time, teachers are colleagues in name only. They work out of sight and hearing of one another, plan and prepare their lessons alone and struggle alone to solve most of their institutional, curriculum, and management problems. (p. 165)

Lieberman and Miller (1990) also describe this "self-imposed and professional sanctioned isolation" when they state that peer relations among teachers are traditionally "remote, oblique, and defensively protective" (p. 160). They point out that the rule of privacy governs peer relations. They argue that although it has been customary for teachers to complain about students and to discuss the news, weather, and sports, surprisingly, it has not been nearly as acceptable for teachers to discuss what actually happens in classrooms from a pedagogical perspective.

A renewed interest in collegiality

In spite of this rather bleak picture of teaching, in the last few decades there has been an increasing emphasis on collegiality, occasioned in large measure by the middle school movement with its emphasis on teaming. When done properly, teaming reduces isolation, provides teachers with regular opportunities to learn from one another, and models the kind of collaboration that teachers, in turn, expect to see from their own students.

But exactly what do we mean by collegiality? Jarzabkowski (2002) describes collegiality as "teachers' involvement with their peers on any level, be it intellectual, moral, political, social and/or emotional" (p. 2). Barth (2001) states that the classic hallmarks of collegiality are talking about practice, sharing craft knowledge, celebrating the success of others, and observing one another engaged in practice.

Little (1990b) goes one step further by identifying four increasing levels of collegiality:

- *Storytelling and scanning* for ideas, which involves teachers sharing anecdotes, griping, and complaining and where the interaction is neither deep nor focused.

- *Aid and assistance,* which involves teachers providing help only when asked, where non-interference is the "name of the game," and deep relationships seldom develop.

- *Sharing of knowledge and resources,* which involves changes in practice but does not involve teachers actually working together.

- *Joint work,* which involves teachers developing deeper and richer ties with each other through activities such as team teaching, collaborative planning, peer coaching, and conducting action research.

Joint work also requires and develops stronger shared responsibility, interdependence, and a collective commitment to improving the quality of teaching. Teachers who work effectively as a team and engage in joint work are not only willing to share supervision duties and planning, but they also develop a set of expectations and obligations toward each other. Main and Bryer (2005) suggest that there are six indicators that teams are actually engaging in joint work:

- Each team member has a clear role and a specific purpose.

- There is an equitable distribution of responsibilities.

- Team members are flexible and are able to adapt to changing circumstances.

- There is regular, open, and honest communication between team members.

- The team has clear and attainable goals.

- The team makes use of the expertise of team members to attain the best possible outcome for students.

However, as straightforward as these indicators may seem, not all middle grades teachers are able to reach this degree of collegiality, and some actually resist any attempt to force them to become willing team members. Why does this happen?

The challenges of collegiality

First, joint work demands that teachers relinquish some of their autonomy when the norms of the team take precedence over their individual preferences. This shift in the balance of autonomy and conformity can make some teachers uncomfortable.

Those teachers who are more individualistic than collaborative in their orientation can find the emphasis on teamwork to be stifling. Others may want the freedom to question the assumptions that their peers are making but feel there is too much pressure to conform and to always accept what the group feels is best. In other words, they resist the kind of "group think" that often occurs when people who have similar responsibilities are expected to work together.

Second, joint work might be seen by some as a method for others to monitor their professional practice rather than as an opportunity to grow professionally. For teachers who are new to the profession, teachers who are struggling, or teachers who lack confidence in their ability to teach, teaming can be perceived as a means by which their inadequacies quickly become public.

Finally, as Main and Bryer (2005, p. 199) suggest, the close interactive and collaborative environment of teaming "can stimulate a paradoxical response that heightens incompatibilities among different personalities, differences in teaching styles, and non-shared pedagogical beliefs." Furthermore, not all members of teaching teams are equally committed to working in a collegial manner.

Although on the surface, most teachers claim that they respect different approaches to teaching, in reality, conflict can quickly develop when teachers with different philosophical orientations are expected to work together. Similarly, incompatibilities often surface when teachers who have different ways of interacting with students are expected to teach side by side.

Given that middle grades teachers are as diverse as the students they teach, the reality is that *who* is on the team often makes a significant difference in how effective the team can be. In other words, the psychology of individual team members often trumps more substantive matters.

Rethinking collegiality

Hargreaves (1994) and Little (1990a) have taken provocative positions in their work on collegiality in teaching, and both make a convincing argument for rethinking our assumptions that the best teaching is collaborative and that the most effective teachers are those who spend a lot of time with their peers. Little (1990a, p. 510) describes collegiality as "conceptually amorphous," and similarly, Hargreaves argues that terms like collegiality are "vague and imprecise…mostly symbolic, a motivating rhetoric in a mythical discussion of change and improvement" (p. 165). He reminds us that:

> Physically, teachers are often alone in their classrooms with no other adults for company. Psychologically, they never are. What they do there in terms of classroom styles and strategies is powerfully affected by the outlooks and orientations of the colleagues with whom they work now and have worked with in the past. In this respect, teacher cultures, the relationships between teachers and their colleagues, are among the most educationally significant aspects of teachers' lives and work. (p. 165).

In essence, Hargreaves asks us to reconsider what we mean by collegiality and the importance that we place on teachers working together in the same physical space. He encourages us to think about those teachers who may find the emphasis on collaboration to be too restrictive and inconsistent with how they think and work best. He challenges us to think about whether or not our enthusiasm for collaborative teacher cultures has disadvantaged some of our most gifted teachers. On this point, Hargreaves argues,

> A system that…cannot accommodate strong and imaginative teachers who work better alone than together, that calls individualists prima donnas and turns creative virtue into non-conformist vice—such a system is a system devoid of flexibility and wanting in spirit. It is a system prepared to punish excellence in pursuit of collegial norms. (p. 182)

But where does that leave middle grades educators who have embraced collaboration as a hallmark of middle grades pedagogy? Does Hargreaves have a point when he refers to mandated collaboration as "contrived collegiality?" How can middle grades teachers and administrators balance teachers' desire for autonomy with the expectation that they will also work effectively as a part of a team?

The following case illustrates how effective teaming and collegiality can sometimes be elusive. It highlights the dilemmas that arise when one member of the team is unwilling to conform to group norms.

Case Study: The Hallway Resident

"I can't stand it anymore," exclaimed Bob Forest, "Marsha is moving Darren back into the hallway again! He's carrying his desk, and he's got all of his work under his arms!"

Sherry Verdin nodded sadly in agreement, "I know; it's getting pretty bad. But what can we do? We're the new kids on the block, remember?"

"Darren can act impulsively at times but he's really not that bad," John Kyle, the veteran of the trio said, "I've had more challenging students than him over the years."

Bob Forest, Sherry Verdin, and John Kyle were teachers at Gregory Middle School, which was in the process of making the transition from a junior high to a middle school. Along with their team leader, Marsha Burbank, these three made up the sixth grade teaching team at the school. Each grade was divided into interdisciplinary teams, teachers were expected to collaborate in the planning and teaching of interdisciplinary units, and team members were expected to adopt a common approach in working with students. However, because this kind of teamwork was still relatively new to many of the teachers, it was only marginally successful and some teams were still experiencing "growing pains."

The principal, Eileen Grafton, had made it clear to her staff that they were not expected to become middle grades experts overnight. She had also explained that change almost always involved compromise and at least a little discomfort as people gradually became accustomed to new ways of doing things. In order to make the transition as painless as possible, Eileen had taken a number of measures to support her staff. She readily sent her teachers to workshops that focused on middle grades teaching strategies, and she now made a point of hiring teachers who had specific middle grades preparation.

In fact, Bob and Sherry were two such teachers. They had been hired straight out of the faculty of education at a local university to replace two recent retirees on the sixth grade team. John Kyle, one of the more experienced teachers on the team, had been a teacher for ten years and had been open to change from the outset—that was just the kind of person John was. On the other hand, Marsha Burbank, the sixth grade team leader, a 20-year veteran, was less than enthusiastic about the changes that teachers were expected to make. On a number of occasions, Marsha had expressed her disdain for the middle grades philosophy calling it nothing more than a "passing fad." Initially, she had tried some of the new middle grades strategies, but each time she had found them wanting. She was convinced that her traditional content-centered approaches prepared students better for high school. She also was convinced that the so-called child-centered methods such as differentiated instruction, cooperative learning, and inquiry-based teaching simply pandered to students' desire to play instead of learn. The word in the staff room was that Marsha missed the days when she wasn't pressured to fall in line with the other 6th grade teachers in the school.

One Friday after school, as usual, John, Sherry, and Bob met at their favorite café across from the school. The three team members found that these regular meeting times were important for unwinding and debriefing. It was also a good time for them to discuss the students that they all shared. As they had done in the past, they invited Marsha to join them but, as usual, she declined.

"I have Darren in my drama class and he is terrific," said Sherry. "He listens and does all of the activities. I told you about the monologue he did two weeks ago. That boy's got talent! I have to admit he has difficulty sitting still in language arts, but that's hardly enough of a reason to send him out of the classroom."

Bob smiled and said, "I don't know. He can drive me crazy sometimes, but that's just the way he is."

"I had to talk to him on Monday," John admitted. "He was hitting one of the other kids with his ruler, but after a brief conversation with him, he was fine.

"Well, he does spend a lot of time in the hallways," said Sherry. "Even the other teachers have noticed that Darren does most of his work there or in the office."

"When I asked Marsha how things were going with Darren, she just huffed and called him a *rude little brat*. That's all she said!" exclaimed Bob. "Sure, I'd like him to settle down more, but I don't think he can help himself."

"Like I said before, in my classes, Darren is pretty manageable," said Sherry, "I just keep him busy and on task."

There was a lull in the conversation and then John interjected, "Eileen must see that Darren is spending a lot of time in the hallway. I hope she doesn't think this is a *team* decision. Do you think she realizes that our 6th grade team is a little dysfunctional?"

"All I know is that Darren is getting really frustrated," Sherry said in an empathetic voice. "The other day, I asked him why he was sitting outside of the classroom and he told me that he didn't know. At first I thought that he just didn't want to explain to me what he had done to get kicked out, but then as I talked to him a little more, I realized that he really *didn't* know why he was there."

"Should we talk to Marsha about our concerns?" asked Bob, looking at John. Knowing that he was the most experienced of the group, John guessed that the younger teachers were looking to him for guidance. "Tell you what…let's make an appointment to talk to Eileen about Darren and about our challenges as a team. We'll talk to her about what we are noticing, and then afterward maybe we'll have a better idea how best to approach Marsha."

"You know how defensive Marsha can get," replied Sherry. "I offered to integrate my survival unit with her environment unit, but boy, did she ever give me the cold shoulder when I made that suggestion! She laughed, shook her head, and wouldn't even listen to any of my ideas."

"Yes, I know what you mean, Sherry. I don't think Marsha is particularly fond of any of us," offered Bob. "Maybe she feels threatened."

"That's possible but maybe she just doesn't buy into the idea of working with other people when she knows she can do the same thing more quickly on her own. Do you think she feels excluded?" asked Sherry.

John Kyle laughed, "Well, she isn't here. We invited her to join us and once again she had better things to do. If she feels excluded, she has no one to blame but herself. She may be our team leader, but she is not even part of the team! We need everyone to be rowing together and she's not even in the boat!" As the three teachers got up to leave, they wondered how their principal would respond when they went to her with their dilemma.

Using theory to inform practice

This case, depicting the interactions of team members Sherry, Bob, John, and Marsha, highlights a number of issues that relate to joint work. What follows is an analysis of the case from the perspective of collegiality.

Over the past few decades, there has been an increased emphasis in middle schools across the country on team teaching and working with colleagues in more collaborative ways. Unfortunately, this "one size fits all" approach may fail to acknowledge that some teachers are not well suited for collaborative work. Take Marsha, for instance. Although she is the most experienced teacher on the 6th grade team and the team leader, she is the most resistant to working collaboratively and the least collegial of the four team members. It makes one wonder how she can be a "leader" when she seems to want "to do her own thing" and not have to bother aligning her teaching practice with those of her fellow team members. Furthermore, she remains unconvinced that middle grades student-centered strategies are pedagogically sound, she has an entirely different approach towards her most challenging students, and as they suspect, she may very well be threatened by the new hires, Bob and Sherry. Some of the questions that arise from this case are: Is the situation with Darren just a symptom of a bigger problem with the 6th grade team? Is Marsha one of those teachers who teaches best on her own, and if so, should she be able to do so in a school culture that obviously values collaboration? Further, how should the principal, Eileen Grafton, respond when the three team members come to see her about their concerns?

First, let's consider what the three other teachers have done to date and what they might do differently. By all accounts, they have tried to include Marsha in their team-based decisions. They have invited her to do some collaborative interdisciplinary planning, and they have invited her to join them for casual team meetings after school. It seems that at every turn, she has turned their efforts down and has retreated more and more into herself. It does not seem that all four teachers have had an open and honest discussion about how they feel about their teaming arrangement. It is unclear whether any of Marsha's ideas are considered when the team is engaged in planning. Marsha may feel outnumbered by the three others who apparently share the same views. If the arrangement is basically a one-way street, then it is no wonder that Marsha is a marginal team member at best.

On the other hand, Marsha does teach in a middle school where the expectation is for teachers to collaborate. Maybe she needs to make more of an effort to try new ideas and to be more open-minded toward the student-centered approaches that her colleagues take. She may miss "the good old days" when she could "call the shots" in her own classroom. Now that she is the most experienced teacher on her team and the team leader, she is being expected to reach out to others in ways that are uncomfortable for her. However, she is in no position to encourage and mentor her younger and less experienced colleagues when she is stuck in the junior high paradigm.

The role of the principal is also important to consider in this case. Although Eileen has demonstrated leadership in putting the structures in place for effective teaming and has encouraged professional development opportunities, she has done less work at the ground level with each team. When John, Sherry, and Bob come to speak to her, it may provide the opportunity to look more critically at all of the teaching teams in the school to see how well they are functioning. There may be other teams struggling with the same kinds of challenges, but they have yet to come to Eileen's attention. Perhaps, on reflection, Eileen will consider how important the composition of interdisciplinary teams may be to their success. She might reconsider how team leaders were selected and choose future leaders based on their commitment to this model of teaching, rather than on seniority.

Eileen may also find that she needs to better prepare her teachers for engaging in joint work rather than assuming that all teachers, if given the chance, welcome the opportunity to collaborate. Maybe Gunn and King (2003) have a point when they argue that being a part of a teaching team can often be complex and contradictory work. As they suggest, "hierarchies can emerge, individualistic tendencies can persist, general consensus can be elusive, and members can be silenced" (p. 191). On the other hand, as Sherry, Bob, and John might attest, when teaming works, not only can it be a rewarding experience for teachers, it can also reap tremendous benefits for students!

Case Discussion Questions

1. What is the role of the principal when a teacher like Marsha is either unwilling or unable to respond appropriately to a student's needs? What advice would you give Eileen to ensure that Darren spends less time in the hallway and more time being productive in class?

2. Although collegiality is one of the hallmarks of the profession, it does require a delicate balance between personal autonomy and institutional conformity. How do we reconcile this basic tension so that teachers can continue to grow professionally without being stifled by ideology or dominant team members?

3. Think about the culture in your own school or school district. How collegial is it? In what ways does the level of collegiality in your teaching situation enhance or inhibit your ability to work with students?

Chapter 4

Identity: Making the Transition from Student to Teacher

Student teaching can be the best of times and the worst of times, to paraphrase the famous opening line of Charles Dickens' *Tale of Two Cities*. Student teachers, ready to negotiate the rite of passage leading to professional certification, usually look forward eagerly to their practica. Nevertheless, a recent report, comparing the clinical training of teachers with that of professionals in six other fields, suggests that the reality of practice teaching does not necessarily live up to students' expectations. The report concludes that "student teachers often give their experience a failing grade, calling it limited, inconsistent, and disconnected from coursework" (Neville, Sherman, & Cohen, 2005). Although student teachers generally rank practice teaching more positively than any other component of their professional education, this report alerts us to the limitations and problems associated with this capstone experience.

Sociological ambivalence in the preparation of teachers

One of the reasons that teacher preparation can be so problematic is that prospective teachers must play two major roles, student and teacher, roles that have different expectations and, at times, may even be in conflict. And these, of course, are not the only roles that student teachers are called upon to play. They also experience demands from the other roles they play, such as son or daughter, mother or father, friend, or tutor. These roles affect not only the values, beliefs, and attitudes that student teachers bring to their teacher identity, but also the actions they will take as classroom teachers. Personal identities exert a powerful influence on professional identities, and these must often be renegotiated as students become increasingly committed to teaching.

The term *sociological ambivalence* is used by sociologists to describe the feelings of uncertainty that arise from the type of conflicting expectations that are inherent in being a student teacher. Sociological ambivalence occurs because faculties of education are rooted in two very different institutions: universities and K–12 schools; therefore, student teachers are expected to integrate potentially conflicting norms and potentially incompatible values from the increasingly complex networks that they develop and the increasing number of people with whom they must work. At the core of the student teaching experience is the question, "How can you be a teacher and a student at the same time?"

The student role includes expectations that a student has something to learn and a willingness to learn it, whereas the teacher role involves expectations that a teacher has something to teach and the ability to teach it. The student role involves an inquiry into the underpinnings of pedagogical and content knowledge, whereas the teacher role requires increasing mastery of professional knowledge, understanding, and skills. The role of the student focuses on developing an individual's cognitive and affective skills, whereas the role of teacher focuses on developing these skills in others. While their professors expect their students to adopt an inquiry stance to current practices in schools, their cooperating teachers often encourage them to "learn the ropes" by following their practices uncritically. Indeed, some cooperating teachers go so far as to tell student teachers to forget everything they have learned in their teacher preparation programs.

Alienation and professional identity

Conflicting role expectations may not be easily resolved because as Kleinman (1981) argues, "Those socialized find that different audiences expect them not only to do different things (role conflict) but also to be different" (p. 62). Moreover, competing role expectations may affect some student teachers differently than others. While some may be able to cope with role conflict and even use it as a springboard for professional growth, others may become alienated because they are unable to connect the expectations of the university with the expectations of the field.

Alienation describes feelings of estrangement from social structures, from other people, or even from oneself. Student teachers who become alienated are less likely to invest the effort necessary to manage their time around academic pursuits or make the effort needed to acquire a professional identity. There have been numerous conceptualizations of professional identity, but most include the five tasks identified by Seeman (1972); becoming certifiably competent in a skill, acquiring an intellectual understanding of a body of knowledge and theory, becoming able to regulate one's conduct according to the norms of the profession, committing oneself to work for its intrinsic rather than its extrinsic rewards, and developing a sense of loyalty to others and the duty of professional exchange. He characterizes professional identity as the opposite of alienation. Specifically, Seeman (1972) suggests that there are five types of alienation (powerlessness, normlessness, meaninglessness, self-estrangement and social isolation) and that each of these is the antithesis of one of the five tasks of professionalization. We argue that these are more accurately described as a continuum on which educators can place themselves at different points at different times in their careers. Such a continuum is shown on the next page.

Professional Identity Continuum

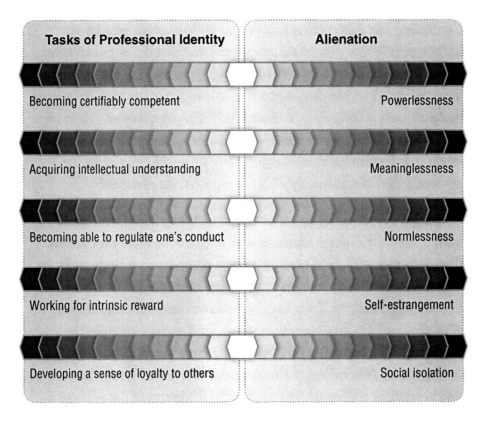

Tasks of Professional Identity	Alienation
Becoming certifiably competent	Powerlessness
Acquiring intellectual understanding	Meaninglessness
Becoming able to regulate one's conduct	Normlessness
Working for intrinsic reward	Self-estrangement
Developing a sense of loyalty to others	Social isolation

Student teachers are expected to form a professional identity by integrating their experiences in universities and schools and by resolving the tensions between conflicting roles. However, some are unable to do so, and they are the ones most likely to develop feelings of alienation. Specifically, student teachers who do not develop feelings of competency as teachers are likely to have a sense of powerlessness; those who are unable to discern the underlying knowledge and theory of their profession may develop a sense of meaninglessness; those who feel they aren't bound by the rules and standards of the university or the teaching profession are likely to experience a sense of normlessness; those who are unable to make a commitment to teaching for its intrinsic rewards may develop a sense of self-estrangement; and those who do not participate actively as members in the wider education community are likely to experience a sense of social isolation.

Resolving the tensions

Given the tensions in student teaching, it is critical that teacher educators both in schools and at universities find ways to mitigate the potential negative effects of sociological ambivalence and alienation on student teachers. Otherwise, there is little to prevent new teachers from succumbing to "a dizzying fall from the heights of unchallenged idealism" (Russell & McPherson, 2001, p.11) and becoming a part of the almost one-half of graduating teachers who leave the teaching profession within five years. A two-year study, *What Matters Most: Teaching for America's Future* (National Commission on Teaching and America's Future, 1996) argues that we must re-conceptualize teaching as an integrated continuum that stretches from pre-service education for novices to continuing education for veterans. To do so, faculties of education and the schools in which student teachers practice need to form partnerships and build in opportunities for student teachers to learn how to be lifelong inquirers into their own practice (National Commission on Teaching and America's Future, 1996; Schulz, 2005; Schulz & Mandzuk, 2005; Wiggins & McTighe, 2006). After all, good teachers need to be good students.

The following case illustrates how understanding identity can help to solve a teaching dilemma. It involves a student teacher in his final year who gets mixed messages from his cooperating teacher and begins to wonder whether or not he should even *be* a teacher.

Case Study: Mixed Messages

West Park Middle School was a medium-sized kindergarten to ninth grade school located in a quiet, mainly middle class suburb of a large metropolitan area. The school was organized into two separate wings, but early years (kindergarten to fifth grade) and middle years (6th through 8th grade) classes shared the gymnasium and library. The principal and the vice-principal jointly administered both areas and the vice-principal, Tom Bergen, also taught 7th and 8th grade social studies.

For the past six years, West Park had been an active partner in the local university's teacher education program. Staff considered it to be their professional duty to supervise student teachers, and they were proud of their record of involvement in the program. Typically, there were sufficient willing volunteers to supervise at least three student teachers each year for their practica. This year was no exception.

The first few days of the practicum were generally used as an observation and a 'get acquainted' period for the three student teachers and their cooperating teachers. During this time, each student teacher began to settle in and become familiar with his or her students and surroundings. One of the three student teachers, Michael Jenkinson, was asked to work with Tom Bergen, the vice-principal. From the moment they met, Tom made it clear to Michael that he was willing to help and offer advice whenever it was needed. As he said to Michael on more than one occasion, "I'll let you do your own thing and give you a hand as you go, but if you want to try some new things, go ahead."

Michael was happy to have a cooperating teacher who encouraged him to take a few risks and to develop his own teaching style. It seemed like Tom was a perfect match for Michael. Tom observed as many classes as he could, given his busy schedule, and gave Michael mainly positive feedback. From time to time Tom complimented Michael on the teaching strategies he used. Once Tom even asked Michael for advice on his own teaching, which, of course, made Michael feel that Tom valued his opinion and that he was an equal. Michael's learning and confidence as a teacher grew as a result.

On more than one occasion, Tom told Michael that he was becoming too chummy with his students. Tom suggested that Michael was getting too personal with his students and that this might create problems for him later on when he had to make difficult decisions. Tom advised him to try to separate the "classroom Michael" from the "out-of-class Michael."

During the remaining weeks of the practicum, Michael tried to act on Tom's advice as much as possible, but he found it difficult to distance himself from the students. Occasionally, he would find himself merely complying when Tom was in the room but reverting to a more informal manner as soon as Tom was gone. Michael really enjoyed teasing and joking with his students and liked to share personal experiences. He really enjoyed his students' company and encouraged his students to seek him out after class. Michael believed that he was engaging his students more effectively in the class work because he was so much in tune with their interests and could relate so easily to their situations.

At the end of the student teaching block, Michael and his faculty advisor met with Tom to discuss how Michael was progressing. As a strong student, Michael had particularly excelled in his "mock teaching" assignments and he was really looking forward to his evaluation. He knew that he had grown a lot from having a real teaching experience. However, it didn't take long before Michael realized that this meeting was going in a different direction. It turned out that while Tom felt that Michael had some potential, he was not overly impressed with the fact that Michael had not changed his behavior with the students and was allowing his students to use his first name and to call him at home. Tom went on to say that he found Michael to be somewhat "immature" because he was behaving more like "one of the boys" than as a teacher.

Although Michael thought he knew who he was as a prospective teacher, he left the meeting and the remainder of the practicum somewhat confused and ambivalent. Was he as far off the mark as Tom thought he was, or did he have what it took to be a strong middle grades teacher? Had he even chosen the right profession? As Michael headed back to the university to complete the term, he had a lot more on his mind than upcoming assignments.

Using theory to inform practice

This case highlights a number of issues that relate to Michael's sense of identity as a student teacher and as a future professional. What follows is an analysis of the case, from the perspective of identity.

In many jurisdictions, cooperating teachers are not paid extra for their work with student teachers. Although not all teachers take on the role willingly, most cooperating teachers, like those at West Park School, believe that, at some level, they have a moral and professional obligation to do so. Indeed, two of the hallmarks of a professional are working for intrinsic rather than extrinsic rewards and displaying a sense of loyalty to others. Mentoring prospective teachers is one form of active participation in the wider educational community. In this case, Michael's cooperating teacher was a busy vice-principal who may not have had sufficient time to mentor his student teacher or to give him specific and helpful feedback. Perhaps Tom needed to be more specific and directive in his comments about Michael's behavior with the students.

Students are required to complete student teaching experiences successfully in order to be certified as teachers. Consequently, universities schedule practicum experiences as part of their mandate to offer teacher education programs. Faculties of education recognize the importance of field experiences but are often challenged to integrate practicum experiences with theoretical courses. For some students, the dissonance they sometimes experience between what they learn in university classrooms and what they experience in the practicum can lead to alienation from the university or from the profession. In this case, there is no evidence that Michael's experiences in the school and his university courses are integrated, nor does it appear that his faculty advisor has played a role in ameliorating Michael's confusion. This is unfortunate because the lessons learned in practice teaching benefit from a critical stance and the lessons learned in university are more meaningful when they have been tested in the realities of the classroom. How can a student teacher develop a clear identity as a teacher without guidance from either the professionals in the school or the university?

For a variety of individual and institutional reasons, far too many student teachers and teachers in their first few years of teaching become disillusioned with teaching. Perhaps it is because so many have been seduced into thinking they have already accomplished the tasks of professional socialization, described earlier; in fact, they may have only served, as Lortie (1975) suggested, "an apprenticeship of observation" watching their own teachers for over 12,000 hours. Michael may have developed unrealistic opinions about his own abilities to perform as a professional teacher because he was not supervised very closely and was too often left on his own.

As the case makes clear, Michael had difficulty processing the mixed messages he was receiving from his cooperating teachers. We think it might have been helpful for Michael to view his dilemma about whether to pursue teaching from an identity perspective. According to Sfard and Prusak (2005) claiming one's identity is dynamic and is "created and recreated in interactions between people" (p.15). In other words, student teachers and new teachers do not develop a single, fixed teacher identity, but rather are engaged in a process of continuous development of their professional identities. Student teachers need to view professional socialization as a process in which they will be revisiting, challenging, and reframing their assumptions, beliefs, and ideas about teaching at the same time they are learning to think, act, and feel like teachers.

Perhaps, the first thing Michael needs to understand is that ambivalence is a natural consequence of trying to make the transition from student to teacher while not being able to fully inhabit either role. Michael has been told by Tom that he needs to separate his student and his teacher role. It appears that Michael is having difficulty distinguishing between developing learning relationships with students and trying to become their friends. He lacks a clear understanding of the teacher role in which he must be both positive and nurturing and still maintain his authority. Student teachers need to find this balance while poised in the precarious position of playing two roles that have very different expectations and at times may even be in conflict with one another. It can be challenging for some student teachers, who are struggling with their own identity, to resist taking sides with their students against authority or to identify more closely with the desires of their students rather than their cooperating teachers.

For student teachers like Michael, the evaluation process can also be a source of ambivalence. Michael seems to think that the evaluation process is one in which he will receive a stamp of approval or rejection. As a new teacher, how can he learn to accept the scrutiny and advice of others to fuel his developing professional identity rather than being overwhelmed by it? Will he continue to get mixed messages about his competence even after he is certified?

Case Discussion Questions

1. Is Michael in danger of becoming alienated from the teaching profession before he even begins? What could the school and the university have done to make his practicum a more satisfying experience?

2. How might the effects of sociological ambivalence and alienation be minimized for student teachers? What kinds of measures do teacher educators need to take to ensure that the professional socialization of new teachers is an encouraging and supportive experience?

3. Review the chart that places the five tasks of professional identity and the five types of alienation on a continuum. As you look at each of the five tasks of professional identity, where do you place yourself on the continuum? Why?

Chapter 5

Community: Understanding Social Capital

Everyone agrees that parents need be more involved in their child's education. Or do they? Historically, parents have been left out of the picture in most middle schools, surfacing mainly to cook hot dogs, contribute to bake sales, and drive students to field trips or sports tournaments. Sometimes, parent involvement becomes associated with "shaming and blaming" and interactions between home and school can be fraught with tension (Sanders & Epstein, 2000). Certainly, not all students, especially those in middle school, want to see their parents in the school. Developmentally, students in the middle grades may perceive parental involvement to be "uncool," especially if it means that parents are intruding on their social space. Not all teachers, for their part, welcome parents to the school or are comfortable working with them. Indeed, some schools that once adopted an open door policy for parents are now struggling to "put the genie back in the bottle" as they try to find a balance between involvement and interference.

Importance of parent involvement

In spite of the inherent challenges, educators strongly believe that parent involvement in the educational process represents a particularly productive form of social capital. Like physical capital and human capital—the tools and training that enhance individual productivity—social capital refers to benefits for individuals and ultimately for society. Unlike the other forms of capital, however, social capital is neither tangible nor transferable, residing as it does in the relationships, networks, and communities in which an individual is a part. The trust that builds up in communities as a result of social capital facilitates the kind of coordination and cooperation that is so evident between parents and educators in effective schools.

Putnam (2000) identifies two distinct, but not mutually exclusive dimensions of social capital—bonding and bridging. Bonding is located in "relations among family members, close friends, and neighbors" (Woolcock, 2001, p. 13), or in other words, the close inward-looking relations between like-minded individuals. At its best, bonding provides close groups, such as school staffs, to grow as professionals in professional learning communities in which they can open their practice to scrutiny by trusted colleagues. At its worst, the very closeness that is prized by some members of a group serves to exclude or isolate others (Portes & Landolt, 1996; Mandzuk, Hasinoff, & Seifert, 2005). In very tight communities, the pressure to conform may be so great that some members feel claustrophobic and resent not being able to voice a contrary opinion for fear of ostracism or sanctions. Taken to the extreme, bonding social capital can result in the creation of gangs whose members dominate others outside their tight circle.

Bridging, on the other hand, is located in relations with more distant friends, associates, and colleagues, or in other words, the more outward-looking relations between people with different interests and goals. Bridging relationships are characteristic of business-like connections, tenuous, relatively specific, and time-limited. To make such connections requires being able to network across social groups in a way that may be very difficult for those who are overly tied to their ethnic, family, or social group(s). On the other hand, those who concentrate too much on making bridging connections may inadvertently weaken their relationships with family, friends, or colleagues. Putnam (2000) captures the distinctions between bonding and bridging by suggesting that, "bonding social capital constitutes a kind of sociological superglue, whereas bridging social capital provides a sociological WD-40" (pp. 22-23).

Whether, it is bonding or bridging, "social capital cannot be understood independently of its broader institutional environment" (Woolcock, 2001, p. 13). Educators, therefore, must always take into account the broader community and context in which schools are situated. In schools, Putnam (2004) argues, educators need to differentiate between social capital generated "inside the walls," including the bonds that are forged among teachers and administrators, and the social capital developed "outside the walls" including the bridges that link schools to the broader community (Putnam, 2004, p. 3). Although both bonding and bridging are seen as critical to student success, educational policymakers are looking with increased interest at the effects of social capital outside the walls of the school.

The positive effects of bridging social capital generated by parent involvement have been widely documented. In fact, the evidence suggests that test scores and dropout rates are better predicted by measures of community-based social capital than by measures of teacher quality, class size, or spending per pupil. When parents are actively involved, students benefit academically, socially, and emotionally. Schools also profit from parent involvement through improved teacher morale, greater support, and higher ratings by community members. Not surprisingly, school-initiated family and community partnerships have been identified as a key characteristic in the cultures of successful schools for young adolescents (National Middle School Association, 2010).

How can schools foster social capital?

Schools can foster social capital through four properties that Coleman (1988) identified as closure, stability, shared ideology, and interdependence. The first property, *closure*, refers to the number of ties within a community or between communities. In small rural schools it is not uncommon for parents and school staff to belong to the same civic organizations and churches and to meet socially as well. In close social networks of this kind, closure occurs through the multiple ways in which parents and schools are connected. By way of contrast, parents in large urban schools may have very few, if any, other associations with one another as students come from widely scattered areas and highly diverse backgrounds. In such cases adolescents may have to take on the roles of being "social brokers" for their families.

The second property, *stability*, which is closely aligned to closure, occurs through the consistent exposure of people to each other over time. Stability is more likely to be present in neighborhoods where there is little mobility or where there is some community agency, such as a church or a recreation center that draws people together on a regular basis. In suburbs, where neighbors may remain unknown to each other, in areas populated by transients, and in communities where linguistic and cultural barriers exist, there are few opportunities for parents and their children to develop social capital. In addition to this lack of stability in many neighborhoods, it has long been noted—and decried—that parents become significantly less involved in their children's education as students enter middle school.

The third property, *shared ideology*, refers to shared expectations and behavioral norms, and the sharing of all kinds of information among like-minded parents and teachers. For example, parents of students with particular interests or abilities, such as band or athletics, often share beliefs in the efficacy of these extracurricular programs and develop social capital as they work together to support these programs financially or as volunteers. In addition, some large middle schools, recognizing the need for students and parents to develop a shared ideology have created "schools within schools" (National Middle School Association, 2010). These smaller structures, commonly known as "houses" or advisory groups, provide students and parents with opportunities to develop shared traditions, symbols, and goals.

The fourth property, *interdependence,* refers to the collaborative partnerships that exist in relationships of high trust. Typically, middle schools are not as successful as elementary schools in developing conditions of interdependence with parents. In order for conditions of interdependence to be created, parents need to be invited to share critical information about their own children and to become active partners in decision making in matters that affect the way the school operates.

Unfortunately, for a large number of parents, developing collaborative partnerships with schools is not a likely option. As Aronson (1996) points out,

> A growing number of parents do not speak or read English well enough to communicate with teachers and administrators. Because of cultural differences, many parents are not familiar with the expectations of their children's schools and don't understand how to go about getting involved, even if they want to. Some parents lack the educational background or skills they feel they need to interact with teachers and staff. For others, their own negative experiences as students make them uncomfortable going to the school. (p. 58)

Often what is interpreted as lack of interest or caring on the part of parents is a cultural predisposition to interpret help at home with interference and disrespect for the teacher. In addition, many working parents have time constraints that prevent them from being involved with the school. Considering that 87 percent of a student's waking hours from birth to age 18 remain under the influence of the home environment, it is essential for schools to acknowledge the significance of parents as educators in the early years and the continued influence they exert on a student's response to schooling.

Unfortunately, parents who are marginalized through poverty, minority status, or cultural, linguistic, or ethnic differences may experience great difficulty in developing bridging social capital with other parents in the school. Epstein (1995) argues that to help such parents, schools need to get out of the "rhetoric rut" in which they express support for parent involvement, but fail to take any action. Schools can increase opportunities for closure and stability by planning meetings, activities, and conferences at times when parents are actually available to attend and by encouraging employers to allow working parents to have greater flexibility in their work schedules. Schools can improve the likelihood of shared ideologies and interdependence being developed by making important school information and decision making open to all parents regardless of their language, ethnicity, or socio-economic background.

School initiatives to increase parent involvement depend not only on the willingness of the school to make it a priority but also on the ability of teachers to work with parents as partners in their students' education. Such preparation needs to be built into teacher education programs so that pre-service teachers learn why it is important to involve parents and develop techniques for working productively with them. Unfortunately, many new teachers report that working with families is largely missing from their teacher preparation (Hiatt-Michael, 2001).

The following case illustrates how social capital can help educators understand the impact of various kinds of parental involvement. It involves a principal and a first year teacher who are caught in a dilemma that forces them to examine the appropriate role of parents in the school.

Case Study: Who Wields the Power, Anyway?

Stratford Middle School was located in Marketville, a large one-factory town that was having difficulty bouncing back from the recession. Marketville was suffering badly from the economic downturn, resulting in some permanent layoffs and a lot of cancelled shifts at the factory. The principal, Jack Degan, knew how important the viability of the factory was to keeping the school open and vibrant, so he worked hard to maintain positive relationships with the town's movers and shakers, particularly those who had children in the school. Jack knew just how important it was to have the right people in the room and at the table when tough financial decisions had to be made. As a long-term resident of the town, Jack knew who to approach, and he was pleased when a number of influential people had responded to his invitation to run for the district school board. Jack was never afraid to ask community members to help out in the school, get involved in fund-raising activities, or share their expertise with students. As the principal, Jack often reminded his staff how important parent volunteers were to Stratford Middle School's success, and he made sure that the Volunteer Tea was considered a highlight of the town's social calendar.

Brad Doyle, who grew up in a large city several hundred miles away from Marketville, was a first year teacher. After he graduated, he was happy to spend the summer at his family's lake home where he relaxed and spent time with his relatives and friends. By mid-August, Brad felt refreshed and eager to start his new job. He arrived in Marketville just in time to find an apartment and get ready to start his teaching career in September. By the end of the second week, he was beginning to feel fairly comfortable, especially with his 6th and 8th grade classes. However, he was still unsure how best to deal with the challenging behavior of some of the students, particularly a group of rowdy students in his 7th grade science class. By the end of September, the behavior of this group had become so unruly that Brad was forced to call Jack for help.

Mr. Degan arrived at the classroom door as Brad was just about to begin his next 7th grade class. In a monotone voice, devoid of any emotion, Jack announced that if the students' behavior did not improve immediately, *he* would be contacting their parents. The ultimatum had the desired effect and Brad was pleased to find that his 7th grade science classes were much more productive.

A couple of weeks went by, and although the behavior of the students had deteriorated a little, it was still a noticeable improvement over what it had been at the beginning of the year. Unfortunately, less than a month after the principal's warning to the class, the same group of students began to disrupt with their raucous laughter once again. Sensing that things were starting to get out of hand, Brad sent four of the loudest students to sit outside the office until he could deal with them properly.

After the class was over, Brad sat down and talked to the students, and after setting the consequences for what they had done, he went inside to talk to Jack, who asked him to fill in the details of what had happened. Brad told him about the students' inappropriate behavior and explained that he wanted to "nip it in the bud" before it escalated and became a serious problem again.

Jack listened as Brad explained what he had done to keep on top of things and then responded, "You're doing just fine, Brad. Just remember that I'll support you if you decide to call a meeting with the parents to address your concerns." Brad left the office feeling empowered but quite unaware of the internal struggle that was going on in Jack's mind as he reflected on the events of the day.

Unfortunately for Jack, Sam Burns, one of the boys Brad had sent down to the office was the son of Harold Burns. Harold was one of the people that Jack was counting on to stand up for Stratford Middle School when the board started to look for ways to cut costs for next year. As someone new to the community and as a first year teacher, Brad couldn't possibly appreciate what might be at stake if Harold believed that his child did not deserve the consequences that had been set.

As Jack gazed out the window at the half-finished football stands, he couldn't stop thinking about the power wielded by parents like Harold Burns. Jack was anxious about whether Harold would see the school's actions as understandable or whether he might expect special treatment for his son. Jack wondered whether he had built up sufficient trust with Harold to navigate the bumpy terrain of discipline. Would doing the right thing for this group of 7th grade students mean one less vote for the school?

Using theory to inform practice

Although parent involvement in schools is generally recognized as highly desirable, this case highlights a dilemma in which a principal is forced to examine social capital from a more nuanced perspective.

Brad Doyle, like other new teachers, generally has no involvement with the school board and little understanding of how the board influences the resources available to his school. Jack Degan, on the other hand, knows all too well that elected board members make policies, oversee and account for the budget, and ensure that the necessary human and physical resources are available to support the ongoing activities of his school. Although effective school boards maintain an arms-length relationship to individual schools and have little or no direct involvement in their day-to-day operations, it is their decisions that determine what can or cannot happen in a school.

In the best case scenario, school boards attract members who bring a wide range of experience to the table and act as unbiased representatives of their constituencies. In the worst case, people who are anxious to push a single issue or agenda, such as the special needs of their own child, or see their election to the school board as a political stepping stone are the ones most likely to seek office. Often, there is a small but influential group of people viewed by the majority as the "in-crowd" who make most of the really important decisions in a community. When this occurs, community organizations begin to look more like "old boys' clubs" that newcomers and more marginalized community members may find difficult, if not impossible, to penetrate. Jack Degan is well aware of the social dynamics in his community. He makes it his business to ensure that the board includes trusted parents who will keep the interests of Stratford Middle School at the forefront, especially in these tough financial times.

Although this case provides us with little insight into who Harold Burns is as a parent, we can certainly understand Jack's concern about the potential of "stepping on Harold's toes." While it is evident that Jack Degan understands the importance of ensuring that he has developed social capital with members of the school board and has successfully promoted the benefits of involving parents in the school, he is also aware that shared ideologies cannot be taken for granted.

Closure, stability, shared ideologies, and interdependence are as important for staff members as they are for parents. Jack is careful not to undermine Brad's authority to manage his students and demonstrated a clear understanding of the importance of bonding social capital. Collaboration, trust, and reciprocal expectations and obligations are unlikely to flourish in schools where there has been little effort to build social capital.

For his part, Brad, as a newcomer to Marketville, has had very little time to become acquainted with its citizens or to develop an understanding of the town's precarious financial situation. As a new teacher, he has enough to think about without worrying about fostering good relations with school board members. However, if Brad is to earn the trust and cooperation of the students and their parents, he will need to learn much more about them and to make a concerted effort to build social capital inside and outside his classroom walls.

There is no justification for treating students differently according to the amount of social capital a parent can draw upon. Aside from violating basic principles of fair play, Brad's classes would be impossible to manage if students perceived that there was any favoritism. To be as transparent as possible with parents, Jack might open up school practices, such as those concerning student conduct, to scrutiny, revision, and discussion. The school might invite parents and students to participate in the creation of a school code of conduct that clearly articulates the roles, responsibilities, and expectations of staff, students, and parents. Once developed, students could be charged with the responsibility for making parents and community members aware of its contents. When policies are collectively developed and thereby become more transparent, schools are less vulnerable to pressure from influential groups or individuals.

Ask yourself if *your* school treats parents as educational partners. What draws parents and teachers together? What drives them apart?

Case Discussion Questions

1. Jack is concerned that his ability to use social capital to facilitate the goals of his school may be jeopardized by his support for his teacher's handling of a student discipline matter. How might he have responded differently?

2. There are both upsides and downsides to the social capital generated by parents, teachers, and administrators. What do you think are the upsides and downsides of involving parents more meaningfully in school operations?

3. Think about your own efforts to build social capital in your school. What attempts have you made to bridge to parents and help students bond with each other? How does the concept of social capital help you understand relationships in your school community?

Chapter 6

Authority: Finding the Balance to Engage Learners

One of the most pressing concerns for teachers is learning how to manage their classes effectively. This involves establishing and maintaining authority in the classroom. Although they must learn the curriculum and the pedagogy related to that curriculum, what really weighs on their minds is whether or not they will be able to manage their students effectively. While this is most pronounced for beginning teachers, it is a continuing challenge for many veteran teachers as well. Lieberman and Miller (1990) emphasize this point when they state,

> The setting of control norms is a necessary part of teaching; it satisfies the need for certainty in an otherwise ambiguous and uncertain world. It also assures teachers of their place in the organization of the school. No matter how effective teachers are in the classroom, all that is ever really known about them in the general organization of the school is whether they keep their classes in line or whether the students are in control. Control precedes instruction; this is a major shibboleth of teaching. (p. 153)

If the setting of control norms is as important as Lieberman and Miller suggest, one might argue that it is perhaps most important in the middle grades when young adolescents feel a need for greater autonomy and become less willing to defer to those in authority. Therefore, many beginning teachers are surprised to find that establishing these norms can be more challenging than they expected. First, most of them lack experience asserting themselves in large groups and are often taken aback when their students do not voluntarily comply with their requests. Second, they are expected to exercise their authority, not only in the private spaces of their own classrooms, but also in the more public spaces of the school. Not surprisingly, beginning teachers often face an uphill battle establishing themselves as legitimate authority figures.

How do teachers establish and maintain their authority and engage their students? We think an important first step to understanding this important question is to clarify what we mean by concepts such as control, power, authority, and engagement, and to do so, our discussion will lean heavily on the work of Clifton and Roberts (1993), Dooner et al. (2010), Marzano and Marzano (2003), Schlechty (2001, 2005) and Spady (1977).

Primary mechanisms of control

In his article entitled, "Power, Authority, and Empathy in Schooling," William Spady (1977) makes important distinctions between three primary mechanisms that teachers use to gain compliance from their students. The first mechanism of control is power or *coercion*. When teachers use this approach in the classroom, compliance is achieved either by threat or by the use of sanctions. In other words, students are forced to do what they have been asked to do; and if they don't, certain resources or freedoms are withheld. While this approach may produce short-term compliance, it also tends to breed resentment and disengagement. Therefore, teachers who want to engage their students and build long-lasting learning relationships with them are well advised not to follow this approach as coercion is generally counterproductive.

The second mechanism of control is *persuasion*. On the surface, this approach appears to be more pedagogically sound because students have a voice in the decisions that ultimately affect them. Students are more likely to comply when they are convinced that certain options are more favorable than others. Nevertheless, this approach has some disadvantages. For example, when persuasion is used almost exclusively, teachers may find that they are constantly negotiating with their students. For their part, students may begin to feel that they should have a voice in almost every decision, whether it affects them or not. Persuasion can be a highly impractical approach resulting in inefficient and unpredictable classrooms. In these circumstances, students may be engaged in gaining control but not in meaningful learning.

The third mechanism of control is *authority*, an approach that Spady (1977) distinguishes from power in two important ways. He states that with authority, (1) students voluntarily comply with the requests made of them, and (2) they at least initially withhold judgment regarding the legitimacy of those requests when they are made.

In other words, authority is a type of legitimate power grounded in a basic sense of trust so students readily comply with their teachers' requests. They make an effort to be engaged because they believe that their teachers have taken an interest in them and have their best interests in mind.

Individual and institutional authority

In their book, *Authority in Schools*, Clifton and Roberts (1993) elaborate on Spady's basic characterization and suggest that there are two main types of authority that teachers can use to gain compliance from their students—*institutional* and *individual* authority. Institutional authority resides within the structures of social organizations such as schools and refers to the rights and privileges bestowed upon members of those organizations. There are two types of institutional authority: legal and traditional authority, and two types of individual authority, expert and charismatic authority.

Authority

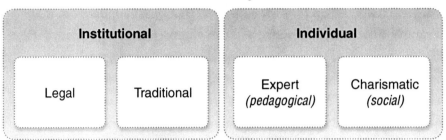

Legal authority is based primarily on the supremacy of the law and refers to the rights, privileges, and obligations of those within an organization. If you think of organizations (such as schools or school districts) as a pyramid, those at the top (such as superintendents and principals) have the most legal authority at their disposal, those in the middle of the pyramid (teachers) have less legal authority, and of course, those at the bottom (students) have the least. Obviously, teachers and administrators who understand and can articulate their responsibilities and obligations to students are well placed to gain the cooperation of those in their charge.

Traditional authority, unlike legal authority, is passed on from one generation to the next. It refers to the "traditional practices that take on an unquestioned, taken-for-granted quality in schools" (Clifton & Roberts, 1993, p. 82). This mode of authority tends to perpetuate the existing social order, it favors schools that have long histories of academic, athletic, and creative excellence and it is exemplified in the plaques, photographs, trophies, and banners found in the hallways of schools that value these kinds of traditions. Teachers are able to use these traditions to make their behavioral expectations explicit. In fact, potential students and their parents are likely to know about some of these traditions even before they set foot in the school.

Expert authority. Although we consider an understanding of institutional authority to be important, it is perhaps more important for teachers to understand individual authority because it is more directly under their control. According to Clifton and Roberts (1993), the first type of individual authority is expert or pedagogical authority, which refers to the degree of expertise that teachers have in the subjects they teach. Pedagogical authority draws upon three kinds of specialized knowledge and skills that have an effect on student engagement: (1) an understanding of the challenges that students experience in mastering content, (2) an understanding of students' developmental levels, and (3) a capacity to use a range of effective pedagogical techniques.

Charismatic authority. The second type of individual authority is charismatic or social authority, which refers to the ability of teachers to meet students' social-emotional needs in a stimulating and engaging manner. It is important to note that teachers who have social authority need not be entertainers or personalities; however, they do need to be able to develop emotional bonds with students. Teachers who engage students are better able to manage classrooms and maximize student learning. The work of Dooner et al. (2010) and Schlechty (2001, 2005) makes the connection between authority and engagement more explicit.

Connecting authority to engagement

Schlechty (2005) characterizes the engaged learner as one who pays attention and shows commitment to an activity because he or she believes that there is value in it. As Dooner et al. (2010) point out, this involves some degree of compliance because the promise of extrinsic rewards or the avoidance of unpleasant consequences can be achieved by getting the job done. Just getting the job done is clearly insufficient unto itself because compliant learners are not always committed to creating meaning from their learning. However, compliant students are more likely to learn than those who are disengaged or those who are refusing to comply as a matter of course. These are students who, as Schlechty (2001, 2005) says, learn to "sleep with their eyes wide open" or rebel by substituting classroom activities with other more entertaining tasks.

On this point, Dooner et al. shed light on the seldom-examined relationship between authority and engagement. They make the case that teachers with a high degree of both pedagogical and social authority are more likely to be successful in engaging a greater number of their students than teachers whose authority styles are less balanced. In other words, neither expertise nor relationship is sufficient unto itself.

The following case illustrates how understanding authority and its relationship to engagement can help to manage a teaching dilemma. It involves a beginning teacher who is having difficulty engaging her students. However, after observing a colleague she begins to re-examine her assumptions about effective teaching and the importance of establishing learning relationships with her students.

Case Study: Questioning Assumptions

Donna Trimble was a first year teacher who had won the gold medal in her graduating class and was looking forward to a long and rewarding career in teaching. In spite of the fact that she was just a beginning teacher, Donna was confident in her teaching abilities. She felt she had a great deal to offer her students because she had an exceptional grasp of both mathematics and science and she was eager to impart her knowledge to them.

Donna spent the summer creating PowerPoint slides and fine-tuning the notes for her lectures. She was sure that this was time well spent because she knew that this kind of detailed attention to content would help her students really understand the concepts. In fact, she was determined that her students would perform better on the standardized tests than any of the other 7th and 8th students in the district. She was also determined not to fall into the trap she had seen so many of her colleagues fall into when they spent most of their time building relationships with their students at the expense of teaching them much of anything.

Donna's year with her 8th grade students at Prince William School had started off well enough, but as she began to prepare for mid-terms, she could feel an ever widening gulf between her and some of her students. As she gazed across the room at the body language of the students in the back row, no one had to tell her that she was losing some of them. She wondered how they could be so disengaged when she found the content so interesting.

She was concerned that they were regularly walking into her class late and were performing poorly on her pop quizzes. Donna had been handling the situation by reprimanding the students and handing out detentions based on the amount of time they were late. However, both the students and Donna knew that this strategy was not having much effect.

Needless to say, Donna felt that she was accomplishing very little with these students, and it was obviously frustrating to those who arrived on time and were ready to learn. Donna knew that Harold Phelps, the physical education teacher was also having trouble with this group of students, but he had a reputation for treating them as if they were primary students and they were understandably fed up. Donna thought about who else was teaching these students and recalled a conversation she had with Alice Petrovsky. Alice had been raving about how creative they were, and how much fun they were having in her civics class. Donna wondered how teachers could have such different experiences with the same group of students. She was curious about whether Alice had been talking about all of the students or just the ones who were always ready to learn so she arranged to visit her class. Alice gladly agreed because she wanted her students to have an audience for the play they had written on the right to bear arms. To Donna's surprise, all of the students, including the group she was concerned about, were prepared, in costume, and fully engaged in the learning experience. She watched as Alice went around the room, speaking individually with each student, laughing at their jokes and coaxing them to do their best. The play was provocative and well written, and it was clear that the students had put a great deal of effort into it. It was obvious to Donna that the students were enjoying themselves and learning at the same time.

Donna wondered if students preferred Alice's social studies classes because they liked the subject, or if they simply preferred Alice as a teacher. To answer this question, Donna found excuses to visit Alice's class a number of times over the next few weeks. Each time, she was struck by Alice's deep knowledge of the students and what motivated them. For the first time that she could remember, Donna began to question her own assumptions about teaching. Maybe she had placed too high a value on test scores and content. Perhaps she needed to concentrate, at least for awhile, on building learning relationships with her students. But then again, how easy would it be for her to change her authority style, given the amount of time that had already passed and the norms that had already been established? She began to doubt whether she even had the capacity to change—after all, she was no Alice!

Using theory to inform practice

Although an understanding of both institutional and individual authority is important, this case highlights specifically how the individual authority of teachers can affect the engagement of students. What follows is an analysis from the perspective of authority focusing specifically on the underlying tension between relationship and expertise.

There is little doubt that establishing and maintaining one's authority as a teacher is one of the most important and yet one of the most challenging aspects of teaching, particularly for those just starting out. It requires the ability to strike a delicate balance between demonstrating expertise in one's subject matter and developing relationships with students as individual learners. We have argued that this balance is critical to being able to engage students in meaningful learning.

In this case, it becomes clear early on that Donna's competence in teaching math and science does not seem to be sufficient. Once she observes how successful Alice is in engaging students, she begins to think more seriously about the role of relationships in learning.

Donna might have taken a lesson from Marzano and Marzano (2003) or Dooner et al. (2010) who talk about providing flexible learning goals, taking a personal interest in students, and using equitable and positive classroom behaviors. In practical terms, this means that Donna needs to involve students more in setting their own learning objectives. Donna might consider giving students choices that go beyond choosing which questions to complete and which colors to use. As she saw in Alice's class, Donna would be wise to acknowledge that her students have important ideas of their own and can demonstrate what they've learned in a wide variety of ways.

Furthermore, Donna needs to take a more active interest in the important events in her students' lives. Her interactions need to engender a sense that her students are valued as learners with unique needs and interests. She needs to move beyond punitive measures such as detentions toward more positive interactions with her students. Finally, Donna would be well-advised to open her practice to trusted colleagues who could observe her teaching and provide feedback about how well she is balancing content and relationship. After all, it is not easy to change one's authority style on one's own, especially when it is grounded in deeply-held beliefs.

Case Discussion Questions

1. In this case, Donna's confidence is shaken by the group of students that she is not able to engage. What do you think has influenced how she currently teaches, and what will need to happen for her to change how she teaches in the future?

2. During your career, there will always be some students who you think could be more engaged in learning. What sources of institutional and individual authority do teachers have at their disposal to cope with the kinds of challenges presented by disengaged students?

3. The best teachers strike that magic balance between demonstrating expertise in content and developing relationships with students. What lessons can you draw about achieving this balance when you look back on the teachers who had the most impact on *you* as a student?

The Four-step Process for Managing Dilemmas

Part Two

1. Describe the dilemma(s) in the case
   and specify who "owns" the dilemma(s).

2. Determine which dimensions
   and underlying tensions apply to
   the dilemmas.

3. Identify alternatives for managing the
   dilemma(s) and consider what criteria
   you will use to evaluate these alternatives.

4. Decide which alternative is the best
   and explain why.

Chapter 7

The Four-step Process and Sample Case Study

Having worked through the five main concepts and their underlying tensions in Part One, you are now ready to take a broader conceptual and practical perspective to the complex dilemmas presented in Part Two. Since dilemmas in teaching are not just about diversity, collegiality, identity, community, or authority in isolation, we need to take a more sophisticated approach that acknowledges the interaction of dimensions and their underlying tensions. As educators, we not only need to understand the theory underlying dilemmas but we also need a practical way to look at alternative courses of action so we can justify the choices we make.

In the final section of the book, you will analyze dilemmas that involve more than one dimension and the underlying tensions. Before that, we will introduce a strategy to manage dilemmas and offer a sample case study entitled "Professional Peer Pressure".

We have found that the following four-step process is a practical, successful approach for working through and managing dilemmas:

1. Describe the dilemma(s) in the case and specify who "owns" the dilemma(s).

2. Determine which dimensions and underlying tensions apply to the dilemma(s).

3. Identify alternatives for managing the dilemma(s) and consider what criteria you will use to evaluate these alternatives.

4. Decide which alternative is the best and explain why.

In complex cases, once you have decided who owns the dilemma and what dimensions and tensions apply, it becomes clear that there are a limited number of alternative courses of action from which to choose. Either knowingly or unknowingly, the act of choosing among alternatives involves applying criteria, the standards upon which judgments or decisions may be based. Which criteria we choose will vary from dilemma to dilemma. In any event, standards or criteria such as those listed below help us to make judgments:

- How important or trivial the matter is.

- How many people are affected.

- How deeply those people are affected.

- How urgent the matter is.

- How sensitive the matter is.

- How the matter affects job security.

- How long-term or short-term the implications of the matter might be.

In the end, you will probably choose a number of criteria that are most relevant to the dilemma that you face. Ultimately, the course of action that you choose will probably not be perfect, but it will be informed by what is most important to you.

Bearing this in mind, as you read the next ten cases, think about what you would do in similar circumstances. What criteria would you use to choose a reasonable course of action in order to manage the dilemma?

Sample Case: Professional Peer Pressure

The early morning sun lit up the sky with a bright mixture of blue and orange. Bill Sigurdsson stood in the sub-zero weather scraping the ice off his windshield. He paused for a moment to look at his neighbor's house. The curtains were parted slightly and Cory, Kevin Fonseca's five-year-old son, was staring at him. The little boy brought his hand up to wave, but the curtains suddenly flew shut. Bill was puzzled at first, but smiled to himself as he went about his business. He figured Cory and his older sister were probably playing a hide-and-seek game. Bill and Kevin were colleagues at Armstrong Middle School and the two teachers usually drove to school together, sharing expenses and stories about the staff and students as they made the commute. Today, however, Bill was on his own as he headed to school early for Track Club.

Bill spent a lot of extra time with sport teams and other school clubs and was always the first to volunteer to spend time with students in need. Because of his warm relationships with students, he was generally considered to be the most admired teacher at Armstrong Middle School. The other teachers appreciated Bill's involvement in school activities and recognized the important role he played in developing a positive school climate. Parents were grateful for Bill's dedication and the large binder stuffed full of thank-you letters that Bill kept in his desk drawer attested to his well-earned reputation. As he drove to school that morning, Bill's thoughts turned to his plans for the rest of the day. However, nothing prepared him for what was about to happen.

Looking grim and resolute, two of his fellow teachers, Greg Parsons and Maria Gonzalez, met him at the front door. Greg spoke up first, "Bill, I'm afraid that you will have to cancel Track Club today." He explained that the teachers at Armstrong Middle School would not be involved in extracurricular activities until the teachers' stalled contract negotiations with the school district were revived. Maria piped in, "We need to get these talks started again! If the district gets pressure from some of the parents, then maybe we'll get some action!"

Bill knew that negotiations had not been going well, but he was sure that things would eventually work themselves out. They always did. The two teachers stood like armed guards waiting for his response. Bill shrugged his shoulders in response and said, "Don't you guys think this is a little rash? Stopping extracurricular activities just hurts the students and our real complaint is with the district. Is this even legal?"

Greg sighed and shook his head, "Look, there is nothing in our current contract that says we have to do any extra stuff! So, if we stop, the district can't do anything about it."

Bill stood silently as Greg and Maria continued to argue why it made sense to cancel extracurricular activities. He couldn't listen anymore. He loved coaching, and he could only think about how much this boycott would affect his students. Bill knew that activities like Track Club kept a number of his students in school and off the streets. For some students, belonging to a club was the only thing that made them feel good about themselves. Out of the corner of his eye, Bill saw Trevor Matthews, a troubled adolescent who epitomized the emotionally fragile kids he was thinking about. Suddenly, Bill blurted out that he had no time for petty union tactics and quickly strode past them to catch up with Trevor.

Later that day, his neighbor, Kevin, stopped by Bill's room. "A lot of people are talking about what you did this morning," Kevin began.

Bill shot back, "I really don't care! The kids come first with me, and I am not prepared to sacrifice them for something I don't believe in!"

"The other teachers don't see it that way! They think that you are just worried about your reputation as a Mr. Good Guy!" Kevin said accusingly.

Bill rose out of his chair. "That's just ridiculous! You know I don't care about that! Look, I have contacted several other schools, and the other coaches think this is a crazy idea, too. On top of that, I don't even remember being given a chance to vote on it!"

Kevin shifted uncomfortably from one foot to the other. "That's true. We decided not to involve any of the coaches in the vote. We know how strongly you guys feel about cancelling extracurricular activities, so we figured it was in your best interest to be able to tell the kids that you had nothing to do with the decision. That way you'd be able to keep their trust and support your colleagues at the same time."

"I don't believe I am hearing this!" fumed Bill, shaking his head in disbelief. "What kind of covert operation are we running here? Last time I checked, this was still a democracy, and I was still working at a simple old middle school! Kevin, some of these kids have enough conflict to deal with in their own lives. School should be the one place they are sheltered from adult disagreements. Can't you guys see the danger in using these students as political pawns to solve a contract dispute?"

"Oh grow up, Bill!" Kevin retorted. "Everything is political! And the sooner our kids understand that, the better!" Kevin paused for a moment to calm down and then continued in a low, steady voice. "Look, I understand your feelings, but we need to stand together. We need to show that we are united during the bargaining process. If just one of us decides to go against the will of the others, it weakens our overall case." Kevin could see that his appeal for solidarity was having little impact on Bill and his face reddened as he continued in a more heated manner, "If you turn on your colleagues now, you should know that a lot of them will be upset for a very long time. Who knows, some of them may not even be interested in carpooling anymore, if you know what I mean." And with that, Kevin turned on his heel and left.

Bill dropped back into his chair and stared off into space. He felt like he was drifting on a large ocean. He kept replaying the scene from earlier that morning when Cory was staring through the curtains next door. What was he doing—spying for his dad? And what was Bill to do now? If he gave into his colleagues' demands, his integrity would be compromised, but if he stood his ground, he would certainly be ostracized. This would take some time to think over. Unfortunately, Bill knew that he didn't have the luxury of time.

Using the four-step process for managing the dilemma(s)

1. **Describe the dilemma(s) in the case and specify who "owns" the dilemma(s).**

   In this case, Bill Sigurdsson, a middle grades teacher and coach, described as an admired, well-liked, and student-centered teacher, finds himself in a no-win situation. Like many middle grades teachers, Bill painstakingly builds positive relationships with troubled adolescents in hopes of keeping them in school. He recognizes that extracurricular activities like the Track Club he coaches fulfill affiliation and self-esteem needs for such students. However, his peers demand that Bill cancel Track Club in order to bring pressure to bear on the district to resolve a protracted contract dispute. Furthermore, Kevin Fonseca, his neighbor and colleague, has warned Bill that there will be serious personal and professional repercussions if Bill doesn't support the union's position.

2. **Determine which dimensions and underlying tensions apply to the dilemma(s).**

   Three dimensions: collegiality, identity, and community, along with their underlying tensions are clearly implicated and interrelated in this dilemma.

   Collegiality. At times, working with others in a collegial fashion requires a special effort to balance the underlying tensions between autonomy and conformity. In this case the dilemma arises, in part, because Bill's sense of autonomy is threatened by the demands of his colleagues to present a united front at the bargaining table. For Bill this call for solidarity creates a struggle between his need to make decisions based on his own experiences and beliefs and the need to accept the role of the union in securing better financial and working conditions through collective action. Whether Bill considers the union's pressure tactics to be necessary to get the talks started again or not, he feels a strong obligation to his students who need extracurricular activities to meet their affiliation and self-esteem needs. Although his personal beliefs and concerns for his students cause Bill to initially reject the prevailing decision to cancel all extracurricular programs, he may be forced to reconsider his position in light of his colleagues' demands to conform.

Identity. Underlying professional identity are tensions created by conflicting role expectations. Like most teachers who enter the profession because of their commitment to students, Bill's professional identity is largely bound up with his role as a mentor. Although Bill has displayed little interest in his role as union member, his colleagues expect him to fulfill this role in the interests of the group. These two roles are inherently conflicting and give rise to feelings of uncertainty, characteristic of sociological ambivalence. On the professional identity continuum, Bill is clearly driven more by the intrinsic rather than the extrinsic rewards of teaching. He gives less consideration to the status of the contract negotiations and the union's call for solidarity than to the needs of his students. It may well be that his job, pay, and working conditions ride on the ability of the union to speak on behalf of all its members, but Bill does not take this into consideration when he chooses to supervise the Track Club. Although Bill does not wish to become socially isolated from his colleagues, he risks doing so because his identity is more tied to the role expectations of being a mentor than those of being a union member.

Community. Bill has obviously invested considerable time and energy in building trusting relationships with students and parents inside and outside of school hours. Although many of his peers admire Bill for his efforts, some, according to Kevin, suspect Bill's motives. In any event, the social capital that Bill has developed with students and parents place him at odds with the demands of the union to use parents as a wedge against the district in their contract negotiations. Bill appears to have little social capital from which to draw among his peers and indeed it is quite likely that the staff will ostracize him if he continues to oppose the cancellation of extracurricular activities. There is no evidence to suggest that Bill has built up any significant social capital with the union either, as he wasn't even allowed to vote on the decision that has so profoundly affected him and his students.

3. **Identify alternatives for managing the dilemma(s) and consider what criteria you will use to evaluate these alternatives.**

Neither the union nor his colleagues are likely to accept Bill's opposition to cancelling extracurricular activities, but the depth of feeling aroused by this dilemma will likely depend on how protracted the negotiations become and the degree to which Bill's peers become unified in their support of the union's position. Sometimes autonomy can result in an individual becoming socially isolated from his or her peers for a short time, but if sufficient social capital has been accrued, the rift will not likely be permanent. In fact, when tempers cool and contract negotiations have concluded, Bill may even gain newfound respect for having stuck to his principles in a tough situation.

As we saw in Chapter 1, managing a moral dilemma such as the one facing Bill involves having a series of losing arguments with oneself. As Bill considers the conflicting expectations of the roles (including mentor and union member) that he plays, the importance he attaches to his individuality and the wishes of the group, and the degree to which he has developed social capital with parents, students, and peers, he may see that the choices before him are limited and that none of them is wholly satisfying:

1. Bill can conform to the union's demands and hope that he has accrued sufficient social capital with students and parents to ride out the temporary interruption of extracurricular programs. In so doing, he will gain his colleagues' support and the union's approbation, but he risks jeopardizing relationships with those students who may neither accept nor understand his motivation.

2. Bill can continue to be involved in extracurricular activities and hope that the social isolation he is likely to suffer will be short-lived. In so doing, his autonomy may remain intact as he honors his commitment to his students, but his loyalty to his peers will be suspect and there may be residual resentment long after the contract dispute has been settled.

3. Bill can seek employment in a non-unionized environment and hope that he will never again be placed in such a difficult dilemma. In so doing, Bill will not have to resolve the sociological ambivalence of his conflicting roles but he will be abandoning the very relationships he has tried so hard to develop and protect.

To manage this dilemma, Bill is forced to make hard choices. How do we make such difficult choices? Either knowingly or unknowingly, the act of choosing involves applying criteria. The criteria we choose will vary from dilemma to dilemma but generally our criteria involve taking into consideration who is most affected by the dilemma or who is most affected by the choices involved in managing it. Our families, for example, may be the most severely affected if we choose to change jobs in order to manage the dilemma. In considering who is most affected, we might ask ourselves which choice affects us the least (or most) ethically, socially, emotionally, and financially and which choices affect significant others the least (or most) ethically, socially, emotionally, and financially. In this way, the choices we make may not be any more palatable or satisfactory, but they will be informed by what is most important to us.

4. Decide which alternative is the best and explain why.

Once Bill has determined his alternatives, he can examine each in light of the criteria that are most important to him. Bill decides that the most important criteria for him is the welfare of his family. He understands that, in the current economic climate, he is unlikely to find work nearby and that leaving the school will mean leaving the city. This is simply not an option since his father-in-law, who lives close by, is becoming increasingly dependent on Bill and his family for support as his health continues to deteriorate. Also, his wife would be terribly unhappy to leave a well-paying job in which she has been given considerable responsibility. Besides, his nine-year-old daughter and twelve-year-old son would be heartbroken if they had to leave their friends.

Having ruled out the alternative to leave the school, Bill is left with two alternatives. He must either support the union or exercise his autonomy and continue to offer extracurricular activities to his students. Upon reflection, Bill decides that he must side with his colleagues so that the contract dispute can be resolved more quickly and because his colleagues have always been there for him. Bill dreads the reaction from his students when he will have to explain his decision but feels confident that they will know that he is sincere in promising to resume practices as soon as possible. He realizes that his students may one day be working in unionized environments themselves and that he can use this opportunity to teach them about the importance of solidarity.

Case Discussion Questions

1. Why do you think Bill's colleagues have taken the action that they have? Is there any other approach that they might have taken with Bill?

2. As a professional, Bill is torn between the claims of loyalty to his colleagues and his commitment to his students. As a professional, Bill is torn between the claims of loyalty to his colleagues and his commitment to his students. Is there any way that he can fulfill his obligations to both his students and his colleagues?

3. In your opinion, should teachers have the right to strike or to withdraw their services? Justify your opinion.

Chapter 8

Case Studies for Practicing the Four-step Process

Case 1: Caught Between a Rock and a Hard Place

The mixture of architectural styles at Northwood Middle School mirrored the make-up of the school population. Most of the students came from mainly well-established middle class homes while a growing number of students came from newly built low income housing nearby. The school was divided into two wings—the older Kindergarten through Grade 6 section and the modern Grade 7 through Grade 9 section. Although the principal was new to the school and had only worked in high schools prior to transferring to Northwood, the vice principal, Greg Miller, had worked at the school for years and had led the movement to create middle grades teaching teams. Greg was responsible for student discipline and for organizing the placements of student teachers from the local university.

Melissa Conroy, was one of three middle years student teachers who were placed at the school for their teaching block. Gustavo Stanton, the eighth grade science teacher, was Melissa's primary cooperating teacher, but she also worked with the other members of the eighth grade team: Sally Longston, the language arts teacher; Chris Pallen, the mathematics teacher; and Bob Hack, the social studies teacher. The team was responsible for teaching three different eighth grade classes: 8A, primarily made up of students of average ability; 8B, with a number of exceptionally strong students as well as a number of students with behavioral problems; and 8C, who were generally considered to be the most challenging class in the entire school. On top of their other problems, many of the students in 8C could not read fluently above the fourth grade level.

Early one morning, about a week-and-a-half into Melissa's first teaching block, Chris approached her to ask a favor. "Melissa, I have an appointment last period and I was wondering if you would mind teaching 8B their math lesson today?"

"Sure Chris. I haven't taught Grade 8 math before, but I think I can handle it. What would you like me to teach?"

"Just show the students how to solve the simple equations on page 42 of the text, and then assign them the problems at the end of the chapter to work on their own or in pairs. Greg is responsible for monitoring the student teachers, so I'll ask him to check in on you once in a while to make sure that everything is going smoothly. He won't mind since his office is just down the hall.

Melissa thought about her day as she began to prepare for the class. In the last three periods, she would have 8C for science, an observation period with Bob's 8A social studies class, and then it would be time for her debut mathematics class with 8B. She was excited about teaching on her own, even if it wasn't really *her* lesson.

During Gustavo's science class, 8C was nearly out of control. Some students were yelling, some students were acting as though they wanted to pick a fight, and a couple of students seemed to be on the verge of tears. Something was definitely going on, and Melissa felt as though this classroom and her career were about to spin out of control. Later on in social studies, she voiced some of her apprehensions to Bob, who minced no words when he spoke of the students in 8C.

"What a real bunch of misfits! They…Well, let's just say most of them shouldn't even be in school," he said. "Kids like Ryan, Aldo, and Toby will never amount to anything. Just tolerate them, Melissa. In my opinion, we give those kinds of kids way too many chances."

"Perhaps," replied Melissa uncomfortably, "but isn't it possible that, given the right environment, these students might actually be successful?"

"You are just a bit naive, Melissa. The reality is that we won't get anywhere with kids who don't want to learn. We have to focus on the few kids who are making an effort and leave the others to fend for themselves."

Melissa was frankly disheartened by Bob's defeatist attitude, but she thanked him for sharing his thoughts and quickly dashed off to prepare for her mathematics class.

Unfortunately, the class did not go as well as she had hoped. 8B, though not as rowdy as 8C, were not behaving well, and Melissa was frustrated. A number of them were really testing her limits. Bob happened to be passing by and before she knew it, he came roaring into the classroom. He began to yell at the class about their disrespectful attitude prompting Shane, one of 8B's most volatile students, to respond with a gesture and a snide remark. Bob raised his voice even further and Shane shot back, "What gives with you, old man?"

"What makes you think that you can speak to me like that?" blustered Bob.

As the argument escalated, Melissa and the rest of the class listened in disbelief. She tried to settle the class down, but her efforts seemed to have virtually no effect. The students were clearly enthralled by the spectacle before them. Shane shook his head in disgust and stood to leave the class, but Bob physically blocked him at the door. Shane's face reddened as he barked out, "Don't you touch me. You have no right to lay your hands on me. Don't touch me, old man, or you'll be sorry!"

"I have the right to do what I need to do to get you out of this classroom!" Bob hissed back.

Bob was propelling Shane into the hallway when he spied Greg, who was coming by to check on Melissa. The vice-principal quickly intervened, sending Shane to the office and addressing the rest of the class. He calmly reminded them to treat Melissa with the same respect they would any other teacher, and the students quickly settled down and went back to their work quietly.

After class, Greg called Melissa into his office. "I'm very sorry to put you in this position, Melissa, but I need to know exactly what happened between Shane and Bob back there in the classroom. Shane is making some serious allegations and you are the only adult who was there to see the whole thing."

Melissa could see immediately that she was about to be put in a very awkward position, and she wasn't at all sure how she would respond. How honest would she be about Bob's attitude toward the students?

Using the Four-step Process to Manage Dilemmas

1. Describe the dilemma(s) in the case and specify who "owns" the dilemma(s).

2. Determine the dimensions and underlying tensions that apply.

3. Identify alternatives for managing the dilemma(s) and consider what criteria you will use to evaluate these alternatives.

4. Decide which alternative is the best and explain why.

Case Discussion Questions

1. A number of factors led to Melissa's dilemma at the end of the case. What were some of these factors and how could they have been avoided?

2. In this case, Melissa is part of the 8th grade teaching team and wants to be seen as a colleague, but she is also trying to carve out her own identity as a beginning teacher. How should she navigate between these competing forces?

3. If you were Melissa and had been placed in a similar situation in which you were the only adult who witnessed the incident unfold, how would you have responded to the vice-principal? Explain.

Case 2: A Breakdown in Communication

Richmond Community School was located in a small city of 35,000 people. The teachers and administration of the school prided themselves on building strong working relationships with students and their families; in fact, some of the school's teachers had even written and published an article about school-community partnerships in *Middle School Journal*. However, building relationships with parents sometimes comes at a cost as the new principal, Jack Parsons, and one of his most promising teachers would soon find out.

One day early in December, Jack received a call from the superintendent informing him that he had received an urgent e-mail message from Mr. and Mrs. Kowalski who had some serious concerns about Majinder Singh, one of Richmond's 8th grade social studies teachers. Mr. Kowalski was an influential businessman who knew all the right people in town and had been a long-standing school trustee, and Mrs. Kowalski was the chair of the PTA for the fifth consecutive year. Although they had always been courteous to Majinder, the young teacher had noticed that they were never reluctant to capitalize on their personal and social relationships to get things done. The superintendent hinted to Jack that rather than asking the parents if they had followed the proper protocols as he normally would have, he was asking Jack to immediately "fix" the problem before it became more widely known that the Kowalskis were unhappy.

In the e-mail, the parents stated that Majinder was neglecting their son Albert's needs: he had made little attempt to challenge their gifted son, and the educational assistant who was supposed to be providing Albert with support for his dyslexia was being pulled away to meet the needs of those students in the class whose problems were severe enough to warrant an Individual Education Plan (IEP). Unfortunately, having been at the school for only a few months, Jack knew little about Albert's needs or his parents, so he called Majinder into his office, told him about the e-mail he had received and asked him if he was aware of the Kowalskis' complaints.

Majinder was shocked at the news; not only had he not heard anything from the parents themselves, but he had taught Albert the year before and felt that he was accommodating Albert's needs through differentiation. He thought that he had developed a good working relationship with the Kowalskis. Majinder explained to Jack that last year, the 7th grade team to which he belonged had determined that although Albert was indeed academically gifted, he had difficulty staying on task, was frustrated with reading, and was becoming increasingly discouraged. That is why Majinder and the educational assistant had created differentiated assignments and a plan to address both Albert's abilities and his disabilities.

However, Albert was now in 8th grade and there were more students with special needs in his class so that his educational assistant provided more support for them and less support for Albert. Majinder thought that this had been made clear to the Kowalskis at the "Meet the Teacher" night earlier that year. To complicate matters, this year Albert didn't seem to be doing as well. He was not submitting assignments regularly and on time, and he was also frequently late or absent.

Jack asked Majinder to read the e-mail again, to conduct an extensive review of how Albert was performing in his class, and to describe what he believed was the problem. Majinder returned to his classroom and began reading the e-mail more carefully. As he did so, he wondered how he had allowed this to happen and why the Kowalskis hadn't spoken to him first.

Majinder began his documentation and quickly realized that, in this semester, Albert had been late 28 times and had missed 12 classes. He had submitted only 18 out of 23 graded assignments and they had not been completed to Albert's usual standard. Majinder knew that Albert had not been doing as well as he should have, but perhaps he hadn't paid enough attention to Albert's performance or the time that he had missed. Majinder realized that Albert's parents had reason to be concerned about their son, but he felt that their accusations were hurtful and untrue. Above all, he felt blindsided and could not understand why Albert's parents suddenly felt compelled to go straight to the superintendent and bypass both him and his new administrator. For his part, Majinder wondered why he had neglected to review his records up to now and why he had fallen so far behind in keeping Albert's parents fully informed.

Albert brought the documentation to Jack and asked what the next step should be. It seemed that the Kowalskis didn't want any input from Majinder, or they would have contacted him personally beforehand. In the meantime, Jack knew that the superintendent expected him to "fix" the situation before it became more serious.

In the end, Jack decided to think about it for a few days before deciding how to respond. He wasn't sure if the school had been serving Albert as effectively as it should have been, or if this was just a case of powerful parents making unreasonable demands. Had Majinder been negligent, and if so, was it because he needed more support to handle the special needs students in his class? Jack could tell that this was going to take a while to sort out, but in the meantime, the Kowalskis were waiting for action to be taken.

Using the Four-step Process to Manage Dilemmas

1. Describe the dilemma(s) in the case and specify who "owns" the dilemma(s).

2. Determine the dimensions and underlying tensions that apply.

3. Identify alternatives for managing the dilemma(s) and consider what criteria you will use to evaluate these alternatives.

4. Decide which alternative is the best and explain why.

Case Discussion Questions

1. One of the things that this case highlights is the importance of regular communication with parents, especially those who have children with specific learning needs. What could Majinder have done differently in his interactions with Albert's parents?

2. Although Albert's parents are justified in being concerned about their son's progress, they bypass the school's normal chain of authority and use their social capital to prioritize Albert's needs over those of the other special needs students in the class. In your opinion, when, if ever, is this course of action justified? Explain your answer.

3. It appears Majinder was overwhelmed by the special needs in his class and consequently dropped the ball in monitoring and reporting on Albert's progress. Should Majinder have initiated steps to place Albert on an IEP? How can you ensure that you don't find yourself facing this kind of dilemma?

Case 3: Degrees of Differentiation

Alhambra Middle School was a K–9 school in a mixed income neighborhood in a large southwestern city. Leon Alvarez had taught there for the past 17 of his 28 years as a school teacher. Approaching retirement, Leon was a well-respected 6th grade team leader who was well-liked by both students and parents. This year, as he had for the past thirteen years, Leon taught both 6th grade science and math classes.

The 6th grade classes were heterogeneously grouped and were generally composed of average to above average ability students with the exception of three of the students: Juan, Andrea, and Roger, who were performing slightly below grade level expectations, and Hernando, who was learning English as a second language. Hernando was performing significantly below grade level, especially in language arts and social studies. Even though these four students were having trouble keeping up with their peers, Leon believed that the best way to help them was to hold them to the same high expectations as every other student in his class. Consequently, he provided them with the same materials, assignments, and tests as everyone else. Leon assessed all of his students the same way, mainly using written assignments, notebook checks, and unit tests to arrive at a final grade.

Julie Jensen, the 6th grade language arts and social studies teacher, had moved to the area in June with her husband and was delighted to have found an opening at Alhambra Middle School, just a ten-minute walk from her new home. When she arrived at the school, Leon gave Julie an orientation to the school and shared his approach to managing diversity in the classroom. He told her not to worry about programming specifically for Hernando, and he did not even mention any difficulties that Juan, Andrea, and Roger would likely experience with 6th grade materials. However, Julie became aware of their difficulties almost immediately, and she began to provide some extra help for them. When she tried to talk to Leon about these students, he told her not to change her style of teaching or evaluation because he did not believe this was necessary and any inconsistency between them would cause problems with the parents.

As a teacher, Julie used many different strategies to try to engage the students in the class. She varied her instruction, alternating between cooperative learning strategies, direct instruction, role play, and class discussions. She encouraged her students to try to answer their own questions instead of just feeding them the answers. Julie felt that she was doing very well considering the challenges. She had already been evaluated once by the principal and the evaluation was very positive. In spite of the differences between Leon's and Julie's teaching styles, they made a good teaching team. Leon seemed pleased with Julie's teaching and expressed no major concerns.

Connie Ruiz had been the vice-principal at the school for three years. She had taught at other schools in the district and had been a principal of a much smaller elementary school before coming to Alhambra. Connie made a real effort to be an educational leader. She had a visible presence in the school and she often made a point of stopping by classrooms to touch base with students and teachers. She also acted as a mentor to teachers who were new to the school and had encouraged Julie early in the year to invite her in to observe and evaluate one of her lessons. Just after Thanksgiving, Julie felt that the time was right so she invited Connie to observe one of her social studies lessons. This lesson incorporated drama and was intended to act as a brief review of the Early Exploration unit on which the class would be tested the next day. Connie had a meeting to attend immediately after the lesson, but promised to meet Julie later in the day to share her observations.

Later that day, Julie met with Connie in her office. They began by discussing the lesson. Connie made a number of positive comments and told Julie how she might improve the transitions between activities. Julie found the feedback valuable and was grateful for Connie's input. Just as she was leaving, Connie asked Julie how she was accommodating the needs of the four students who were clearly performing below grade level. Connie made some suggestions about how Julie might vary the reading materials for these students in the future. By the end of the conversation, Julie began to realize that simply varying the type of instruction for the whole class was not the same as differentiating to ensure that all of the students could meet the outcomes. She wondered whether she should consider modifying the upcoming test and decided to keep Connie's suggestions in mind when she planned her next unit.

Before she left for the day, Julie asked Leon for advice about modifying the social studies test for the four students so they would be challenged at their own reading level. As he had done before, Leon maintained that he didn't think that any modifications were necessary and that the test results reflected the diverse abilities in the class. Julie could tell that there was no point in pursuing the matter any further with him. However, she was left wondering what to do with the fact that her vice-principal and her team leader did not see eye to eye on this crucial matter.

She was beginning to think that Connie was right, that students should not suffer poor grades in a class like social studies simply because they had difficulties in reading or writing. On the other hand, maybe Leon had a point. Would modifying the test actually lower the expectations she had for her less able students and was that what she wanted to do? After some thought, Julie still didn't have any answers to these questions, but she knew she would have to try to find them if she was to resolve the conflicting expectations of her team leader and her vice-principal.

Using the Four-step Process to Manage Dilemmas

1. Describe the dilemma(s) in the case and specify who "owns" the dilemma(s).

2. Determine the dimensions and underlying tensions that apply.

3. Identify alternatives for managing the dilemma(s) and consider what criteria you will use to evaluate these alternatives.

4. Decide which alternative is the best and explain why.

Case Discussion Questions

1. Why didn't Julie tell Connie that Leon had specifically told her not to differentiate her instruction and evaluation? What would have been the consequences for her, for Leon, and for their relationship if she had?

2. Connie expects the teachers at Alhambra Middle School to differentiate instruction, but Leon prefers to treat all students the same. How might Julie navigate between these two contrasting views of how to address diversity in the classroom?

3. In this case, Leon takes a traditional approach to teaching, holding high expectations for all students regardless of their instructional needs. What would students in your class stand to gain or lose if you took this approach?

Case 4: What's Wrong with You, Coach?

Champlain Middle School was located in a sprawling, new subdivision built mainly for middle and upper income residents. In the past two years the school population had exploded from 265 to 687 students, putting pressure on all of its resources and calling for changes in the usual procedures. One of these changes affected interscholastic sports. The increase in population meant that the physical education staff had to double the number of teams because the school district had adopted a no-cuts policy for their middle grades interscholastic teams. Although the staff was in favor of giving more students the opportunity to play in competitions and develop their skills, they knew that this might be a tough sell to a community that prided itself on the strength of its volleyball teams.

Drew Fishman was an experienced physical education teacher and a well-respected girls' volleyball coach. Knowing how important it was to keep everyone informed, she called a meeting of the three teachers who had volunteered to be coaches, interested 8th grade girls, and their parents to discuss the upcoming volleyball season. As Drew was explaining what a no-cuts policy was and how the growth of the school meant that they would be fielding two teams, she was interrupted by one of the parents.

"Don't you think we know what you're doing?" challenged a woman near the back of the room. "Obviously the girls will be split into two teams based on their ability to play volleyball. Who do you think you are kidding? That's how it always is."

Some of the parents started nodding in agreement. Drew was expecting this question. It had come up repeatedly in previous meetings with parents whose children were involved in other interscholastic sports teams.

"I understand your concern," replied Drew. "Over the years, you and your children have become accustomed to being involved outside of school in sports teams that are formed solely on athletic ability. However, we will be keeping track of how often each girl attends and how hard they work. Ability level will be just one factor when we form the teams and not the most important one."

"What if my daughter can't attend all the practices? Are you telling me that she might not be able to play?" sneered one of the fathers.

"We have no problem accommodating any student who wants to improve her skills but you are right in saying that girls who do not attend practices regularly will not get as much playing time," Drew responded. She could tell from the amount of murmuring in the room that this new approach was not going to satisfy everybody.

Drew fielded a few more questions about transportation, fees, practice times, tournament locations, and equipment before the meeting came to an end. As she left the gym that evening, Drew was confident that the majority of the parents were with her.

Before the first tournament, Drew created a matrix of all the students and entered the information related to each girl's attendance, how hard each one had worked during practices, what she had contributed to the overall team effort, and her skill level. As Drew examined the matrix, she immediately became aware that, in spite of their efforts, she and the rest of the coaching team had inadvertently created an imbalance between the two teams.

"No matter how we add up the numbers" she said with concern, "quite a few of our most skilled players will be on one team and more of our weaker players will be on the other."

"Well, everyone knew how the teams would be selected so we need to stick with what we said we would do," asserted one of the assistant coaches.

"It would look even worse if we changed our criteria mid-stream, wouldn't it?" added another.

From her experience, Drew knew that when teams are selected, there is always a danger that some parents will respond emotionally. In this case, she was concerned that parents might blame the coaches for stacking the deck and making one team significantly stronger than the other.

Drew walked nervously into the gymnasium of De Soto Middle School for the first volleyball tournament of the season. But, as the day progressed, she could see that the criteria they had used were working. She could see the stronger athletes supporting the weaker ones and as a result, both teams were becoming more cohesive. As the tournament came to a close, she was proud and relieved to see that both teams had ended up in the quarterfinals.

Her relief was cut short the next morning when she picked up the phone and heard Claude Reimer's angry voice accusing her of knowingly dividing the teams unfairly. He went on to say that there were mostly winners on one team and a bunch of losers on the other. He wanted to know why his daughter Cindy had been placed on the weaker team when she was obviously one of the school's star players. "What's wrong with you, coach?" he asked angrily. He continued by asking Drew how she could live with herself knowing that she had probably ruined his daughter's chances to ever play at the high school level and compete for prestigious college scholarships. By the time he hung up Drew was shaken and upset. Mr. Reimer had made her question her philosophy about the place of team sports at the middle grades level. She firmly believed that she had a professional duty not only to ensure that the most gifted players were challenged but also to give anyone who wanted to play the opportunity to participate in competitive sports.

Drew wondered why coaching needed to be so complicated and why it seemed to touch so many nerves. Why was it that some parents simply did not accept a coach's right to make decisions? She was tired of the constant barrage of criticism by what she saw as increasingly empowered parents and began to wonder if it was time to throw in the towel.

Using the Four-step Process to Manage Dilemmas

1. Describe the dilemma(s) in the case and specify who "owns" the dilemma(s).

2. Determine the dimensions and underlying tensions that apply.

3. Identify alternatives for managing the dilemma(s) and consider what criteria you will use to evaluate these alternatives.

4. Decide which alternative is the best and explain why.

Case Discussion Questions

1. Given how important volleyball is to this community and how the district enforces a no-cuts policy, what other approaches could Drew have taken to select her teams?

2. Do you agree with having a no-cuts policy? Do you think it results in a balance between equity and excellence as it is designed to achieve? Why or why not?

3. If you were Drew, how might you respond to parents like Mr. Reimer, who do not agree with your philosophy and question your right to make decisions as a coach or as a teacher?

Case 5: The Disturbing Letter

Brighton Middle School was a suburban middle grades school of about 650 students located near a large city in the Northeast. Students came mainly from ethnically diverse middle-class homes. It was obvious from the newsletters, website, and student-written plays performed each year that Brighton was a school that celebrated diversity, used interdisciplinary teaching, and maintained open communication with parents.

One of Brighton's newest teachers was Anika Sorensen. It was her third year teaching, but her first year at Brighton. Although trained as a middle grades teacher, Anika's first position was teaching five classes of eighth grade social studies. After two years in that traditional junior high setting, however, Anika felt so stifled that she applied for a transfer to a sixth grade teaching position at Brighton.

After an enjoyable interview in which she talked about wanting to teach integrated units and having the opportunity to teach according to middle grades philosophy, the principal, Joel Steinberg, offered Anika the position. Because she was to teach social studies, math, and language arts, Anika spent a large portion of her summer preparing for the next school year. Part of her preparation involved research on the history of North America's indigenous people. She worked diligently to prepare integrated lessons that would instill deep respect and appreciation for diverse native cultures.

On a rainy Friday morning at the end of September, Anika took a deep breath after she had finished a lesson on the Mohawk people. In the few quiet minutes she had before the hallways would be once again filled with adolescents rushing to class, she walked around her classroom. She looked at the painted plaster diorama of a Mohawk village that Ashley and Susan had carefully assembled for their presentation later that day. A smile crossed her face as she looked at Robbie's efforts to make leather moccasins, which looked more like a pair of misshapen punching bags than footwear. Each of her students' projects showed a lot of effort. Anika was convinced that her students were learning a lot more than the curricular objectives by creating models and artifacts based on primary research.

However, when Anika returned to her desk at the back of the classroom, her smile quickly faded. As if drawn by a magnet, her eyes went immediately to the letter she had received earlier that day. She picked it up and slowly read it once again:

> *Dear Mrs. Sorenson,*
>
> *Our family is very proud of our heritage and we believe that your unit on North America's native people does not represent our true history. Our people have been oppressed for too long. I want Andy to learn about what really happened to our people and not be forced to swallow some "white" version of it. I will be watching very closely to see how you teach this material and I will be talking to Mr. Steinberg about it, too.*
>
> *Mabel Crowchild*

Anika remembered the look Andy had on his face when he delivered the letter to her. Being a quiet and shy boy, he had just walked up to her first thing that morning, handed her the envelope, and hurried away without a word. She had opened it promptly and read the letter. Not quite understanding what the letter implied, Anika read it several times. Distressed, she went straight to her mentor, the 6th grade team leader, Carl Green.

He read the letter and began to smile knowingly. "I guess I should have warned you about Mrs. Crowchild," Carl said.

"I had Jordan, her older son, a few years ago, and she was very vocal then, too. Mrs. Crowchild is just one of those parents who needs to put teachers on notice that she is watching you but that's as far as it goes."

"I don't know, Carl," Anika said apprehensively. "She sounds like she means business. Do you think I should talk to Joel about it?"

Carl gave Anika a big grin and said, "That's up to you but if I were you, I would just ignore the note and get on with your teaching."

The next morning, Anika stopped by Joel Steinberg's office.

"May I talk to you for a minute, Joel?" Anika inquired from the doorway.

Her principal smiled warmly from behind the mounds of paper on his desk, "Sure! How are things going, Anika? Sorry I haven't been up to your classroom yet. I hear from Mrs. Frost that you're in the middle of a really good unit on the native people of North America."

"Well, actually, that's why I need to speak to you." She handed Joel the note from Mrs. Crowchild.

Joel read the letter, and sighed audibly. "Well, I guess I'm not surprised by this note. Mrs. Crowchild has been a consistent voice in this school about what she considers to be the revisionist history taught in schools today. She is comfortable talking to me so I could phone her, if you like. However, I think *you* should talk to her. Why not tell her about the wonderful things you are doing in your classroom, and how you are teaching in a way that honors her people? I'll back you up 100 percent."

"Thanks, Joel, you have no idea how much your support means to me."

For the next two days, Anika tried to contact Mrs. Crowchild. She left messages and asked Andy if his mother had received her messages. After a while, Anika began to wonder if Carl had been correct that Mrs. Crowchild was not interested in taking the issue any further.

Then on Thursday, Mrs. Crowchild called the school. Anika's conversation with her was brief and polite. She didn't even mention the letter, but instead, she chose to talk about Andy's grades. At the end of the conversation, Anika invited Mrs. Crowchild to come to her class later in the week to watch the group presentations on the Mohawk people. Mrs. Crowchild was noncommittal but said she would see what she could do about coming.

Anika stared out of the rain-spattered window that Friday morning and wondered whether she *was* teaching history from a white perspective. As a teacher, she had relied on textbooks and other sources that were largely written from the perspective of the dominant culture to which she belonged. Without an extensive background in history, how could she ever ensure that the information her students used for their research reflected what had actually happened? As the buzzer sounded to begin the afternoon, she realized that she had just been skimming the surface of history and that, in the future, she would need to dig much deeper.

Using the Four-step Process to Manage Dilemmas

1. Describe the dilemma(s) in the case and specify who "owns" the dilemma(s).

2. Determine the dimensions and underlying tensions that apply.

3. Identify alternatives for managing the dilemma(s) and consider what criteria you will use to evaluate these alternatives.

4. Decide which alternative is the best and explain why.

Case Discussion Questions

1. How did Anika's reaction to Mrs. Crowchild's letter differ from the reaction of her colleagues?

2. Anika's professional identity includes a commitment to lifelong learning and the constant questioning of her own practice. Given

what we know about this young teacher and her diverse classroom, did Carl and Joel offer Anika the right kind of collegial support? Why or why not?

3. What would you do if, in the course of your teaching, you began to question your subject matter expertise and the authenticity of your sources?

Case 6: What Does It Mean to Be a Professional?

Rockford Middle School was located in a predominantly lower middle class neighborhood in a large urban center in the Midwest, serving a population of 400 fifth to eighth graders. Most of the parents worked hard at blue-collar jobs and were supportive of teachers at the school. Although the teachers seemed committed to their work and to the students, Rockford did have one ongoing problem that a new student teacher would soon uncover.

Eve, a 23-year-old student teacher from a local university, was excited to be at Rockford for her first teaching block. She believed that she had the potential to make a difference in the lives of young people and she could see immediately that there were lots of students who needed extra help. When Eve arrived at Rockford, she was introduced right away to Jan, a charming 7th grade teacher who would be acting as her mentor. Jan was 27 years old and had been teaching for the past six years at the school. The two women seemed to hit it off right away. Jan was pleased to have Eve in her class because she felt that she was open to new ideas and because she always appreciated another pair of hands in a classroom where many of the students had special needs. Eve's first impressions of Jan were very positive. It was evident that her cooperating teacher was well-liked by everyone, colleagues and students alike. Eve felt that she was lucky to have such a good role model to mentor her into the profession.

By Thursday of her first week, Eve was already feeling comfortable in her new surroundings, and she was especially pleased with the positive working relationship that she and Jan were developing. That day after school, Jan asked Eve if she wanted to join the 7th grade teaching team and some other members of the staff for some social time after school on Friday. Eve readily accepted the invitation, anticipating the opportunity to do some networking and hopefully, to make some new friends.

Friday afternoon finally arrived and the school day came to an end. Once all of the students had left, Eve began focusing on the evening ahead. As she was packing up her teaching materials, she reflected on the past week. She had learned a lot about the school, the curriculum in the middle grades, and the students she would be teaching for the next five weeks.

When she arrived at the restaurant, she immediately spotted Jan and sat down beside her. Jan introduced Eve to the other teachers on the 7th grade team and a few other members of the staff at Rockford whom Eve had not yet formally met. With the introductions over, Jan resumed what she had been saying to the others about her students.

"What a day!" Jan began. "I could hardly wait until it was over so I could have a few stiff drinks. Some of my new students, John and Barry, were really getting under my skin today. At one point, I felt like choking them both. I think those kids are going to be nothing but trouble so we all better watch out for them. We won't be taking any guff from them, will we?"

The other teachers laughed and nodded in agreement. Eve was taken aback by Jan's blunt language and her negative attitude toward some of her students. She noticed that Jan appeared to have a strong influence on the opinions of the other teachers around the table. Eve listened attentively to what Jan and the others were saying about those boys and about some other students. Eve couldn't help but feel that what was being said was inappropriate, particularly in a restaurant. After all, they were in a public place just a few blocks from their school and they were discussing issues that she thought should only be discussed in private, in more objective ways, and only with those who really needed to know. She wondered how the parents of these students would feel if they had been in the restaurant and overheard Jan's comments. Feeling increasingly uncomfortable, Eve remained quiet and then slipped away as soon as she could.

All weekend, Eve thought about what she had seen and heard in the restaurant. She felt uneasy about the unprofessional attitudes that some of the teachers had taken and the way their tone had become increasingly sarcastic as they continued to drink. Eve was taken aback by what she considered to be unprofessional behavior by the staff and was particularly disturbed by seeing a side to Jan that she wasn't sure she liked. However, she was determined not to jump to conclusions and eventually, she put the event out of her mind and prepared to start fresh on Monday morning.

Eve was somewhat anxious when she arrived at school because she wasn't sure whether Jan had been offended by her abrupt departure from the restaurant. However, Jan acted as if nothing unusual had happened and the morning went very well. The next day, as Eve was getting ready to leave for home, Jan told her that Peter, the school counselor, was having a party on Friday at his house and that Eve was invited to come. Reluctantly, Eve accepted the invitation keeping in mind what had happened in the restaurant the week before

When Eve arrived at the party on Friday evening, most of the staff members were already there, including the principal. As she began mingling with the other guests, Eve found herself relaxing in the company of some of the older teachers who went out of their way to make her feel welcome. She enjoyed listening to their stories about why they became teachers and what they enjoyed most about their teaching careers.

Around 10:30 that evening, these older teachers began to head home and Eve was thinking about doing the same, but she was hoping to speak to Tim Hutton, the principal, before she left. Spying him over in the dining room, Eve made her way over and started a conversation with him about that morning's school assembly. However, just minutes later, Tim excused himself and moved over to the table where Jan was pouring herself another drink and regaling the other teachers with embarrassing stories about her students and their parents.

Eve quickly decided to thank Peter and his wife and leave before she started to feel uncomfortable again. As she made her way out of the door, she wondered why, once again, Jan was sharing inappropriate information about students so freely. Eve couldn't understand why the principal or the other teachers failed to call Jan on her disrespectful behavior; in fact, they seemed to be encouraging her. There was certainly a disconnect between what she was seeing and hearing and the unprofessional behavior that she had been cautioned against in her university lectures. Eve wondered how she was supposed to develop a positive professional identity when her role models seemed to represent the antithesis of what good teachers should say and do.

As a student teacher, Eve knew that her success depended to some extent on being able to conform to the culture of the school. However, at times like this, she began to question whether teaching was even the right profession for her. She did not want to lapse into unprofessional behavior like Jan and the rest of the team, but at the same time, she wondered whether the standards she held for the teaching profession were unrealistic and perhaps, even, a bit unfair. After all, she asked herself, "Aren't teachers' private lives their own?"

Using the Four-step Process to Manage Dilemmas

1. Describe the dilemma(s) in the case and specify who "owns" the dilemma(s).

2. Determine the dimensions and underlying tensions that apply.

3. Identify alternatives for managing the dilemma(s) and consider what criteria you will use to evaluate these alternatives.

4. Decide which alternative is the best and explain why.

Case Discussion Questions

1. In your opinion, how does Eve's experience at Rockford highlight the fine line that teachers walk outside the classroom when they share stories about their students and their families?

2. Will Eve prevent herself from becoming alienated from the profession? If she conforms and adopts the behavioral norms of her colleagues, how will Eve prevent herself from feeling ambivalent and becoming alienated from the profession? What are the personal and professional costs if she doesn't?

3. During the course of your career, you may occasionally encounter teachers who say and do things that you think are inappropriate and unprofessional. How will you address these people directly or navigate around them?

Case 7: Trial by Fire

Valley Middle School was located in a suburban area of a midsized city in the Northwest. Because many of the students were from families who were transferred on a regular basis, parents were somewhat reluctant to become involved in the daily activities of the school.

This year, Joan Mosienko had been transferred to the school as the new principal. An excellent communicator, she was determined to work with parents to tighten up on some of the discipline problems that she had been warned about. She was well aware that the school had a reputation for being plagued by social problems, but she felt up to the task. Joan was highly respected in the district and was well known for being firm and being able to "get the job done."

As she reviewed the classes, one stood out as the most challenging. The problem in 6A stemmed mainly from the combination of students who had been placed in it. With her trained eye, Joan could see that the class was composed of the most troubled students from the 5th grade mixed in with another smaller group of students who were academically gifted. She wondered how any teacher could hope to address the needs of the students in this class without the aid of an educational assistant.

It turned out that Elaine Darby was one such teacher, and though she was having some of the same difficulties that the other teachers were having, 6A was functioning under her warm and consistent direction. Unfortunately, at the end of September, Elaine informed Joan that she would be going on maternity leave at the end of December. Joan knew that it was going to be a real challenge to find someone strong enough to replace Elaine. The new teacher would not only have to relate well to middle grades students but also be energetic, firm, and able to differentiate instruction for the diverse learners in the class, three of whom were on Ritalin, two of whom who had anger management problems, at least five of whom were reading between a 3rd and 4th grade level, and a handful of others who could easily handle high school curricula.

Even at the best of times, it would be difficult to find the ideal teacher for 6A, but these weren't the best of times for finding teachers, and based on its unsavory reputation, Valley Middle School was hardly anyone's first choice. By the end of October though, Joan had completed the interviews and was prepared, although somewhat reluctantly, to hire Mandy Markus as 6A's new teacher. Although Mandy seemed to be a pleasant enough young woman, Joan was concerned that she might not have enough depth in either the 6th grade curriculum or in differentiating instruction to meet the range of needs in that class. Joan was honest with Mandy and told her that 6A was a challenging class and that meeting the students' needs would tax her resources. Mandy understood but she was just glad to have a job. She had graduated from a local university two years earlier, and all she had been doing was substitute teaching. She was happy to have been offered this term position which she hoped would lead to a full-time job the following year.

Early in January, Mandy arrived for her first day with 6A. Before long, her students started to arrive, and immediately Mandy could tell why Valley Middle School students had a reputation of being difficult. Many of them came in cursing and wrestling with one another, and it was only 9 o'clock! The students who seemed ready to learn were clearly overpowered by the others. Mandy spent the day trying to get acquainted with her new students, and at 4 o'clock she reassured herself that they were just excited about having a new teacher and that the class would settle down the next day.

By the end of the week, Mandy saw no real improvement, and she left the school wondering if she had done the right thing in accepting this position. If she were honest with herself, she had never really felt comfortable with kids this age, and although she was trying to learn, she wasn't prepared to teach the 6th grade curriculum or to address the special needs in the class. Joan had told her that she should allow time for students to get to know her and that it usually took awhile for students to accept a new teacher. At this point, Mandy was not convinced that they ever would.

One afternoon as Mandy was teaching math, things really got out of hand. She was used to having to wait for middle grades students to settle down, but she had been waiting for 15 minutes. Throughout the day, many of the students had been squabbling with one another, and they were having a hard time paying attention. After turning out the lights and telling them to put their heads on their desks, she still didn't have silence. Students shouted out, made rude remarks, and refused to keep silent. Mandy was not about to raise her voice. Finally, she decided to contact Joan, who arrived immediately and stood outside the classroom door, listening to Mandy pleading for her students' cooperation. Suddenly, she pushed open the classroom door and yelled, "Stop!" in a very firm and intimidating voice. All of the students froze. Joan told them that their behavior was unacceptable and that it was going to have to change. She told the class that the next step would be to call in some of their parents to follow them from class to class, and if necessary, she would see to it that they would lose privileges at school and even at home. As they listened to Joan's words, the class remained very quiet. Joan told them that if she had to intervene again, she would not hesitate to carry out her promises. As she left the room, she asked Mandy to see her at the end of the day.

The rest of the day went more smoothly for Mandy. The students kept their voices down, although many were still not very productive. Mandy couldn't help worrying that Joan would think she was incompetent for having to call her to gain control of the class.

At the end of the day, Mandy dismissed her students and took a deep breath as she made her way anxiously to Joan's office. She really didn't know what to expect but hoped that she wouldn't be blamed for the behavior of her class.

"How are you doing, Mandy?" Joan asked with concern. "You know, I really feel for you."

"Well, to tell you the truth, I am very upset about today's mess. This type of behavior happens every day, and I just don't know what to do anymore."

"It's clear that you really have your hands full. Most teachers wouldn't have been able to do as well as you have," said Joan, soothingly.

"Funny you should say that, Joan, because I certainly don't feel that I am doing a good job. I get their attention for about three minutes before something else happens, and then they're off again. I've tried giving them prizes, free time, and extra gym time but nothing seems to work."

"I know how hard you are trying, and it's not your fault. The problem is that someone was asleep at the switch last year and allowed kids who should have been separated to be placed in the same class and now we are paying the price. If I could, I would move some of those students, but at this time of the year that really isn't an option. The parents would be up in arms in no time!"

"I understand that," sighed Mandy, "but in the meantime, how do I control them enough to actually teach them something?"

"Keep doing what you're doing and if you have to, remind them of the drastic measures I proposed. Let them know we are serious about bringing in their parents," replied Joan.

"I hope that works, but I have to say that they still didn't accomplish very much this afternoon," Mandy admitted.

"Well, it takes time to change bad habits, Mandy. You just have to keep at it. Send any of the problem kids to me whenever you have to, even if it happens six times a day. I want them out of the classroom and away from the few that do want to work."

"Okay, I will," replied Mandy hesitantly.

"I'll be by tomorrow to check on things, okay?"

"Sure. Thanks, Joan. I really appreciate your support."

Mandy went home feeling glad that her principal was supporting her, but uneasy about the fact that nothing had actually been resolved. She knew in her heart that she wasn't making the connections with her students that she needed to be making and that she was still playing catch up with the curriculum. She was also aware that the level of engagement in the class was low, especially among the strong academic students whose needs weren't being met at all. Mandy knew that she couldn't send ten students a day to the office and that she needed to gain more control of her class. As she unpacked her marking for the evening, she wondered what she could do to turn things around. How on earth was she going to make it to the end of the year?

For her part, Joan wondered if she had made a mistake hiring Mandy as the teacher for 6A. She knew that Mandy had good intentions, but she also knew that she had to find other ways to support her new teacher without continuing to intervene and, in the process, eroding what little authority Mandy had. Joan knew that a teaching assistant in the class might make all the difference to an inexperienced teacher who had been parachuted mid-year into a difficult class. How could she make the case to the superintendent that she needed a teaching assistant for 6A when the previous teacher managed without one?

Using the Four-step Process to Manage Dilemmas

1) Describe the dilemma(s) in the case and specify who "owns" the dilemma(s).

2) Determine the dimensions and underlying tensions that apply.

3) Identify alternatives for managing the dilemma(s) and consider what criteria you will use to evaluate these alternatives.

4) Decide which alternative is the best and explain why.

Case Discussion Questions

1. If Joan is successful in making her case for a teaching assistant for 6A, what new challenges lie ahead for Mandy? How does this change reflect the kind of support that Joan will have to provide?

2. This case illustrates the complexity of teaching. Even if a teacher had been hired who was strong in pedagogical and social authority, is it likely that effective teaching and learning would occur in this class? Besides issues of authority, what other factors work against teacher and student success?

3. Soon after beginning her new teaching position, Mandy realizes the magnitude of the challenge she has accepted, and she begins to wonder whether she has what it takes to turn the class around. What would you do in her position?

Case 8: Seeking Attention the Hard Way

Booker T. Washington School was an average-sized K–8 school located in a middle-class neighborhood. Generally speaking, teachers had good relationships with their students and their parents, and behavioral problems were relatively rare. Students tended to enter the school in kindergarten and remain there until 8th grade, moving along the grades with the same cohort. All of the students knew each other well and they were extremely comfortable in the school environment and with each other.

Rachel Monahan, the 8th grade teacher, had just graduated from a nearby university. The majority of her class of 24 students had little difficulty with the curriculum, but a few of them were struggling with basic reading and math concepts. One of these students, Marcelo, was new to the school and, as the staff later discovered, he had not been in a regular classroom for the past five years. Before arriving at the school, he had attended small, male-only classes aimed at helping students with impulsive behavior. Rachel knew that Marcelo's parents had recently divorced and that he was now living with his father during the week and with his mother on the weekends.

Marcelo was certainly having a very difficult time adjusting to his new situation. In particular, he had problems controlling his outbursts, and he would spit and use profanity whenever he was upset about something. At the beginning of school, his peers were amused by his attention-seeking behavior and even egged him on. However, as time passed, his classmates became increasingly intolerant and were now completely disgusted with his disruptions. Rachel found that she had to continually interrupt her teaching to remind Marcelo to calm down, take a seat, or stop talking. Unfortunately, these reminders had little effect and finally, Rachel sent him to the principal's office.

When Marcelo returned from the office, Rachel asked him what had happened and, in his words, "Nothing" had. After school, Rachel went to see Meredith Greenspan, the principal, to find out for herself. Meredith recounted what Marcelo had told her about his home life and how hard it was to fit into his closely-knit class. Rachel asked her what consequences she had established to deal with Marcelo's disruptions. Meredith replied that she had told Marcelo that his disruptive behavior was unacceptable but, based on the circumstances, she was prepared to take a positive, supportive approach with him. Rachel pointed out that Marcelo's disruptive behavior was not just a one-time occurrence. He was continually interrupting her class. Meredith was sympathetic to Rachel's concerns and said that next time, Marcelo would be held more accountable.

The following week, Marcelo's behavior deteriorated even further. Rachel tried everything she could think of to engage him in learning, but nothing seemed to work. She told him that his behavior was unacceptable; she tried moving his seat so that he was working beside some of the more patient students, and finally she tried isolating him at the back of the room. When all else failed, Rachel sent Marcelo back to the office.

The next day started out well. Marcelo was fairly quiet during his first class. He didn't really accomplish anything, but at least he wasn't disrupting the rest of the class. Rachel began to think that, perhaps, Meredith's soft approach was working. However, these thoughts were short-lived. By lunchtime, Marcelo was once again doing everything possible to gain the attention of his peers. Once again, Rachel found herself exhausted from investing so much of her time and energy into this one student at the expense of the others in the class. By the end of the day, she decided to approach Meredith once more to ask for ideas on how to deal with Marcelo more effectively. She suggested that Rachel try to ignore Marcelo's behavior and encourage the class to do likewise.

The first thing the next morning, Rachel sent Marcelo to see the principal as they had agreed. While he was away, Rachel opened up a general class discussion about attention-seeking behavior and the importance of focusing on what people do right. One of the students mentioned Marcelo's name, and Rachel took the opportunity to suggest that everyone do their best to ignore his disruptions and try to focus more on his positive behaviors. Her students agreed to try.

Meanwhile, Marcelo was explaining to the principal and the guidance counselor that his classmates only paid attention to him when he created a fuss. They tried to explain to him that this kind of attention was not exactly what Marcelo needed. They went on to suggest that he should watch the students he liked and try to behave more like they did.

That day went more smoothly than most of the previous ones. The students did their best to ignore Marcelo's minor disruptions and so did Rachel. She tried to concentrate on what Marcelo did well and to comment positively each time. Perhaps it was because his classmates were not reacting as they usually did or because he was enjoying the praise he was getting for controlling himself, but Rachel could see that Marcelo was less disruptive.

Then out of the blue, less than a week later, Marcelo began throwing his pencils around the room and cursing at the top of his lungs. Rachel was shocked. She had begun to think that they had turned a corner, but once again, she had no choice but to send Marcelo to the office. Meredith told him to calm down and think about what had caused him to react so strongly. Marcelo finally explained that one of the boys had been whispering about him behind his back. For the life of her, Meredith could not understand why this had triggered such a violent reaction. It was becoming clear to her that taking a positive, supportive approach was not going to be quite enough to help this troubled student or his teacher.

Using the Four-step Process to Manage Dilemmas

1) Describe the dilemma(s) in the case and specify who "owns" the dilemma(s).

2) Determine the dimensions and underlying tensions that apply.

3) Identify alternatives for managing the dilemma(s) and consider what criteria you will use to evaluate these alternatives.

4) Decide which alternative is the best and explain why

Case Discussion Questions:

1. It appears that the staff at Booker T. Washington had very little information about Marcelo when he arrived. He had been attending a segregated classroom, and it is unclear what transition plans, if any, had been put in place to make his integration into a regular classroom a smooth one. What might the school have done differently, if they had known about his academic and personal history from the beginning?

2. In this case, Marcelo, a troubled boy, is engaged in disruptive attention-seeking behavior that interferes with his own and others' learning. This creates a dilemma for his teacher who is torn between the demands of excellence and equity. Is excellence compromised when we mainstream troubled students like Marcelo into the regular classroom? Explain.

3. If you had a troubled, attention-seeking student like Marcelo in your classroom, what other strategies might you use to help him?

Case 9: Walking a Fine Line

Jeff Henderson was in his final year of his teacher education program at a local university. His first year of the program had gone very smoothly, and he had done extremely well in both of his student teaching blocks. He had been fortunate to be assigned to a school in an affluent suburb of his hometown in the Midwest. Students were largely drawn from supportive families and stable homes, and Jeff had few class management problems.

However, his second year placement looked very different. Jeff was assigned to the 6th grade classroom at Farley Junior High School, located in the middle of a poverty-stricken neighborhood. Many students struggled with unstable and unsupportive home environments, and a significant number came from immigrant families who were facing the additional challenge of learning English. The school was well-known for being rough and the word in the school district was that if you could teach at Farley, you could teach almost anywhere. Anxious about his lack of experience in dealing with classroom management problems, Jeff wondered whether he would be up to the task.

As the placement progressed, Jeff understood why other people had warned him about teaching at Farley. It was indeed a very challenging environment but he loved every minute of his practicum. There were certainly plenty of problems, behavioral and otherwise, but he was surviving, thriving, and learning. He had quickly established a good rapport with his students, and most of the initial classroom management issues were quickly fading. In fact, the class was slowly beginning to feel like a community in which students felt free to discuss even sensitive issues openly.

Jeff particularly enjoyed working with students who were learning English as an additional language. He felt that his experience at Farley was invaluable for helping him work with second language learners and understanding the challenges faced by immigrant families. He started a before-school program for students who were experiencing difficulties and many of his new English language learners were regularly showing up for help.

One morning, as Jeff was marking some spelling tests, one of his students, Mufaro, shuffled into the room. Mufaro was experiencing major problems in all of the core subjects, but most of his difficulties could be attributed to the language barrier. He had only moved from Sudan a year before, and in spite of the hardships he had undoubtedly experienced, Jeff knew him to be a generally well-mannered, happy student with a perpetual smile on his face. But not today. Jeff could tell by the way Mufaro was acting that something was terribly amiss.

Jeff greeted Mufaro and asked him how things were going and he responded by saying that they weren't too good. Apparently, his mother had slapped him really hard that morning. Jeff had read the file on Mufaro during his orientation, so he knew a little about the family situation. Mufaro's father had disappeared almost immediately after the family had arrived in the city. As a result, Mufaro's mother was left with three young children, without a job, and with virtually no family support. Still, the woman was working hard to improve her situation by going to language classes offered by a local adult education center. Jeff had seen nothing in the report to suspect that Mufaro was being physically abused. After further discussion, Jeff learned that he had neglected to do his chores, and his mother had slapped him twice on the side of the head. Jeff could see that there was, indeed, a welt on the side of his face.

Jeff was unsure of what he should do next, but he knew that he was obligated to do something. It was painful to see one of his students in obvious distress. He was angry with Mufaro's mother for inflicting physical punishment on the boy, but he didn't think that this was really a case of child abuse. Jeff realized, however, that he had an obligation to report the boy's disclosure immediately to his cooperating teacher, Doug Barkman. At that point, Jeff was certain that Doug would take over and do whatever was necessary to address the problem.

To his surprise, when Jeff was finished relating what had happened to his student, Doug did not assume responsibility for telling the authorities. Instead, he told Jeff to report what happened to Cy Proznik, the vice-principal. As Jeff left for the office, Doug warned him that he would probably be expected to handle the situation on his own.

When Jeff met with the vice-principal, he was assured that he had done the right thing by going to his cooperating teacher and to the administration. Cy told Jeff that this had happened once with Mufaro the year before. Like Jeff, he believed that these were isolated incidents and probably reflected different cultural norms concerning discipline rather than abuse. However, once a disclosure had been made, an adult had no choice but to report the incident to the appropriate authorities. Jeff asked Cy whether he would have to report the situation on his own and the vice-principal confirmed what Doug had told him. As the adult in whom Mufaro had confided, Jeff would be expected to take responsibility and make the call to the local child protection agency.

Jeff walked to the staff room flooded with apprehension. In his heart, he knew that he was doing what was legally right, but it didn't feel quite right morally. What would happen if his actions created an even more unstable environment for his student in the future? Would his actions break apart a family that had been already fragmented and result in separating Mufaro from his mother? Why was this left to him, anyway? After all, he was only a student teacher.

Using the Four-step Process to Manage Dilemmas

1) Describe the dilemma(s) in the case and specify who "owns" the dilemma(s).

2) Determine the dimensions and underlying tensions that apply.

3) Identify alternatives for managing the dilemma(s) and consider what criteria you will use to evaluate these alternatives

4) Decide which alternative is the best and explain why.

Case Discussion Questions

1. In this case, Jeff has no choice but to report Mufaro's disclosure to the authorities, but he worries about the repercussions. What might happen to Mufaro as a result of his disclosure?

2. Parents have a right to discipline their children in any manner they choose as long as there is no physical harm involved. Should schools be concerned with equity when dealing with parenting styles or should they take cultural differences into account? Why or why not?

3. What would you do if one of your students disclosed a similar event to you? How would you walk the fine line between what is required by law and what your instincts are telling you to do?

Glossary

adaptations

    strategies used by teachers to increase the chances that their students will be academically successful (e.g., giving students more time, arranging for alternate settings for testing, and enhancing audio or visual delivery)

alienation

    feelings of estrangement from a social structure, from other people, or even from oneself

apprenticeship of observation

    conscious or subconscious acquisition of skills, dispositions, and beliefs consistent with a future role

authority

    legitimate power exercised by teachers who have earned the trust, respect, and willing compliance of their students

backward design

    approach to instructional planning in which the first step is to identify the learning outcomes, the second step is to determine what form of assessment will demonstrate that outcomes have been met, and the third and final step is to plan learning experiences that will enable students to meet the outcomes

bonding

    close, inward-looking relations between like-minded individuals

bridging

    broad, outward-looking relations between people with different interests and goals

closure

    the multiple ways in which networks of people may be connected to each other

collaboration
> joint work of individuals whose professional learning and satisfaction is enhanced by working with others

collegiality
> sense of trust and interdependence that evolves among co-workers

community
> interconnected parents, educators, and others who work together to maximize student learning

differentiation
> process of modifying content, processes, products, or the learning environment to address student diversity

dilemmas
> problematic situations for which there are no ideal solutions

diversity
> range of cultural, linguistic, religious, socio-economic, social-emotional, and ability levels found in most of today's classrooms

engagement
> degree to which a student pays attention and shows commitment to an activity because he or she believes that there is value in it

equity
> outcome of laws and policies that, when enforced, should guarantee fair treatment and access to resources and programs for all students

excellence
> characterizes a school that sets high academic expectations and standards and makes consistent efforts to help students reach their goals

inclusive classrooms
> classrooms in which necessary changes are made to accommodate the diverse needs of students

individual authority
> authority (pedagogical and social) based upon an individual's attributes

institutional authority
> authority (legal and traditional) based on the social structures of schools

interdependence
> the collaborative partnerships that exist in relationships of high trust

interdisciplinary teams
the common middle grades practice of grouping teachers together who teach different subjects but who share the same groups of students

legal authority
authority based on the supremacy of the law and the rights, privileges, and obligations of those within institutions

mainstreamed classrooms
"regular" classrooms in which students with special needs spend part or all of the school day

norms
formally or informally agreed-upon patterns of behavior within social organizations; they may be enforced through social sanctions

pedagogical authority
authority based on the expertise teachers have in the subjects they teach and their ability to plan and implement engaging instruction

persuasion
giving students a voice in decision making and allowing them to negotiate various aspects of classroom life

power
managing student behavior through threats or the use of sanctions in order to achieve compliance

primary mechanisms of control
managing student behavior by using power, persuasion, or authority

problems
problematic situations for which there are identifiable solutions

professional identity
degree to which a person has internalized the values, beliefs, and attitudes of a profession

roles
patterns of behavior related to the statuses or social positions that we occupy

role conflict
competing demands made on an individual in the fulfillment of his or her multiple social roles

shared ideology
    set of shared expectations, behavioral norms, and increased access to information developed or adhered to by like-minded people

social authority
    authority based on a teacher's ability to stimulate and engage students and earn their trust and respect

social capital
    benefits that accrue as a result of the connections among individuals

sociological ambivalence
    state of uncertainty that results from conflicting role expectations related to a person's membership in different social structures

stability
    extent to which group membership is consistent over time

tracking
    streaming of students into programs/classes according to measures of intelligence or achievement

traditional authority
    authority afforded to teachers based on traditional practices or historically unquestioned rituals

References

Chapter 1

Beynon, C., Geddis, A., & Onslow, B. (2001). *Learning-to-teach: Cases and concepts for novice teachers and teacher educators.* Toronto, Ontario, Canada: Prentice-Hall.

Clifton, R. A. (1989). Knowledge and mythology in teacher education. *McGill Journal of Education 24*(3): 267-279.

Katz, L., & Raths, J. (1992). Six dilemmas in teacher education. *Journal of Teacher Education, 43*(5), 376–385.

Kleinfeld, J. (1992). Learning to think like a teacher: The study of cases. In J. H. Schulman (Ed.), *Case methods in teacher education.* New York: Teachers College Press.

Lampert, M. (1985). How do teachers manage to teach? Perspectives on problems of practice. *Harvard Educational Review, 55*(2), 178–194.

Lampert, M. (1986). Teachers' strategies for understanding and managing classroom dilemmas. In M. Ben Peretz, R. Bromme, & R. Halkes (Eds.), *Advances of research on teacher thinking* (pp. 70-83). Lisse: Svets and Zeitlinger.

Room, A. (1985). *Dictionary of confusing words and meanings.* London: Routledge & Kegan Paul.

Strike, K., Haller, E., & Soltis, J. (1988). *The ethics of school administration.* New York: Teachers College Press.

Chapter 2

Barth, R. (2001). *Learning by heart.* San Francisco: Jossey-Bass.

Borba, M. (2001). *Building moral intelligence: The seven essential virtues that teach kids to do the right thing.* San Francisco: Jossey-Bass.

Colorosso, B. (2004). *The bully, the bullied, and the bystander: From pre-school to high school—how parents and teachers can help break the cycle of violence.* New York: Harper Collins.

Gould, H. (2004). Can novice teachers differentiate instruction? Yes, they CAN! *New Horizons for Learning.* Retrieved April 26, 2010, from http://www.newhorizons.org/strategies/differentiated/gould/htm

Hess, M. A. (1999). Although some voice doubts, advocates say differentiated instruction can raise the bar for all learners. *NEA Communications.* Retrieved December 12, 2005, from http://www.weac.org/Home/Parents_Community/differ.aspx

Jonas, M. (2007, August 5). The downside of diversity. *New York Times.* Retrieved March 12, 2008, from http://www.nytimes.com/2007/08/05/world/americas/05iht-diversity.1.6986248.html

Kulik, J., & Kulik, C. (1991). Ability grouping and gifted students. In N. Colangelo & G. Davis (Eds.), *Handbook of gifted education* (pp. 178–196). Boston, MA: Allyn & Bacon.

Lupart, J. (1999). *Inching toward inclusion: The excellence/equity dilemma in our schools.* Pan-Canadian Education Research Agenda Symposium. Retrieved August 7, 2009, from www.cesc.ca/pceradocs/1999/99lupart_e.pdf

Noddings, N. (1999). Caring and competence. In G. Griffen (Ed.), *The education of teachers* (pp. 205–220). Chicago: National Society of Education.

Oakes, J., Selvin, M., Karoly, L., & Guiton, G. (1992). *Educational matchmaking: Academic and vocational tracking in comprehensive high schools* (No. R-4189-NCRVE/UCB). Retrieved December 11, 2009, from http://www.rand.org/pubs/reports/2007/R4189.pdf

Oberti v. Clementon, 995 F.2d 1204 (3rd Cir. 1993).

Olweus, D. (2003). A profile of school bullying. *Educational Leadership, 60,* 12–18.

Putnam, R. D. (2007). *E pluribus unum:* Diversity and community in the twenty-first century: The 2006 Johan Skytte Prize Lecture. *Scandinavian Political Studies 30*(2), 137–174.

Robbins, L. (2007). Equity vs. excellence: Is education still a zero-sum game? *Peabody Reflector. 76*(2), 17–21.

Robertson, T. S., & Valentine, J. W. (1998). What is the impact of inclusion on students and staff in the middle school setting? *NMSA Research Summary, 14.*

Sapon-Shevin, M. (2000). Schools fit for all. *Educational Leadership, 58*(4), 34–39.

Sergiovanni, T. (1992). *Moral leadership: Getting to the heart of school improvement.* San Francisco: Jossey-Bass.

Tomlinson, C. (1995). *Differentiated classroom instruction for advanced middle school students.* ERIC Digest # E536. Reston. VA: ERIC Clearinghouse on Disabilities and Gifted Education (ERIC Document Reproduction Service No. ED389141)

Tomlinson, C. A., & George, P. S. (2004). Teaching high ability learners in an authentic middle school. *Middle School Journal 35*(5), 7–11.

Tomlinson, C. A., Moon, T. R., & Callahan, C. M. (1998). How well are we addressing academic diversity in the middle school? *Middle School Journal, 29*(3), 3–11.

Wiggins, G., & McTighe, J. (2005). *Understanding by design* (2nd ed.). Alexandria, VA: Association for Supervision and Curriculum Development.

Wolfe, P. (2001). *Brain matters: Translating the research to classroom practice.* Alexandria, VA: Association for Supervision and Curriculum Development.

Chapter 3

Barth, R. S. (2001). Teacher leader. *Phi Delta Kappa, 82*(6), 443–449.

Gunn, J. H. & King, M. B. (2003). Trouble in paradise: Power, conflict, and community in an interdisciplinary teaching team. *Urban Education, 38,* 173–203.

Hargreaves, A. (1994). *Changing teachers, changing times: Teachers' work and culture in the postmodern age.* New York: Teachers College Press.

Jarzabkowski, L. (2002). The social dimensions of teacher collegiality. *Journal of Educational Enquiry, 3*(2), 1–20.

Lieberman, A., & Miller, L. (1990). The social realities of teaching. In A. Lieberman (Ed.), *Schools as collaborative cultures: Creating the future now* (pp. 153–163). New York: Falmer.

Little, J. W. (1990a). The persistence of privacy: Autonomy and initiative in teachers' professional relations. *Teachers College Record, 91*(4), 509–536.

Little, J. W. (1990b). Teachers as colleagues. In A. Lieberman (Ed.), *Schools as collaborative cultures: Creating the future now* (pp. 165–193). New York: Falmer.

Main, K., & Bryer, F. (2005). What does a good teaching team look like in a middle school classroom? In B. Barlett, F. Bryerm, & D. Roebuck (Eds.), *Stimulating the "action" as participants in participatory research* (pp. 196–201). Brisbane, Australia: Griffith University School of Cognition, Language, and Special Education.

Chapter 4

Kleinman, S. (1981). Making professionals into "persons:" Discrepancies in traditional and humanistic expectations of professional identity. *Sociology of Work and Occupations, 8*(1), 61–87.

Lortie, D. (1975). *Schoolteacher: A sociological study.* Chicago: The University of Chicago Press.

National Commission on Teaching and America's Future. (1996). *What matters most: Teaching for America's future.* Retrieved August 8, 2003, from http://www.nctaf.org/documents/WhatMattersMost.pdf

Neville, K., Sherman, R., & Cohen, C. (2005). *Preparing and training professionals: Comparing education with six other fields.* Finance Project. Retrieved May 16, 2007, from http://www.financeproject.org/Publications/preparingprofessionals.pdf

Russell, T., & McPherson, S. (2001). *Indicators of success in teacher education: A review and analysis of recent research.* Paper presented at the 2001 Pan-Canadian Education Research Agenda Symposium, Laval University, Quebec, QC. Retrieved April 9, 2007, from http://www.cesc.ca/pceradocs/2001/papers/01Russell_McPherson_e.pdf

Schulz, R. (2005). The practicum: More than practice. *Canadian Journal of Education, 28*(1 & 2), 147–167.

Schulz, R., & Mandzuk, D. (2005). Learning to teach, learning to inquire: A three year study of teacher candidates' experiences. *Teaching and Teacher Education, 21*(3), 315–331.

Seeman, M. (1972). Alienation and engagement. In A. Campbell & P. Converse (Eds.), *The human meaning of social change* (pp. 467–527). New York: Russell Sage Foundation.

Sfard, A., & Prusak, A. (2005). Telling identities: In search of an analytic tool for investigating learning as a culturally shaped activity. *Educational Researcher, 34*(4): 14-22.

Wiggins, G., & McTighe, J. (2006). Examining the teaching life. *Improving Professional Practice, 63*(6), 26–29.

Chapter 5

Aronson, J. Z. (1996). How schools can recruit hard-to-reach parents. *Educational Leadership, 53*(7), 58–60.

Coleman, J. S. (1988). Social capital in the creation of human capital. *American Journal of Sociology, 94*(Supplement), s95–s120.

Epstein, J. (1995). School/family/community partnerships: Caring for the children we share. *Phi Delta Kappan, 76*(9), 701–712.

Hiatt-Michael, D. (2001). *Preparing teachers to work with parents* (Report EDO-SP-2001-2). Washington, DC: ERIC Clearinghouse on Teaching and Teacher Education. (ERIC Document Reproduction Service No. ED460123)

Mandzuk, D., Hasinoff, S., & Seifert, K. (2005). Inside a student cohort: Teacher education from a social capital perspective. *Canadian Journal of Education, 28*(1&2), 168–184.

National Middle School Association. (2010). *This we believe: Keys to educating young adolescents.* Westerville, OH: Author.

Portes, A. & Landolt, P. (1996). Unsolved mysteries: The Tocqueville files II: The downside of social capital. *The American Prospect, 7*(26), 18–21.

Putnam, R. (2000). *Bowling alone: The collapse and revival of American community.* New York: Simon and Schuster.

Putnam, R. (2004). Education, diversity, social cohesion and "social capital." Raising the quality of learning for all. Proceedings of the OECD Education Ministers' Meeting retrieved August 8, 2008, from www.oecd.org/dataoecd/37/55/30671102.doc.

Sanders, M., & Epstein, J. (2000). The national network of partnership schools: How research influences educational practice. *Journal of Education for Students Placed at Risk, 5,* 61–76.

Woolcock, M. (2001). The place of social capital in understanding social and economic outcomes, *Canadian Journal of Policy Research, 2*(1), 11–17.

Chapter 6

Clifton, R. A., & Roberts, L. W. (1993). *Authority in classrooms.* Scarborough, Ontario, Canada: Prentice-Hall.

Dooner, A.M., Mandzuk, D., Obendoerfer, P., Babiuk, G., Cerqueira-Vassallo, G., Force, V., Vermette, M., & Roy, D. (2010). Examining student engagement and authority: Developing learning relationships in the middle grades. *Middle School Journal, 41*(4), 28-35.

Lieberman, A., & Miller, L. (1990). The social realities of teaching. In A. Lieberman & L. Miller (Eds.), *Teachers: Their world and their work* (pp. 153–163). Alexandria, VA: Association for Supervision and Curriculum Development.

Marzano, R., Marzano, J., & Pickering, D. (2003). *Classroom management that works: Research-based strategies for every teacher.* Alexandria, VA: Association for Supervision and Curriculum Development.

Schlechty, P. C. (2001). *Shaking up the schoolhouse: How to support and sustain educational innovation.* San Francisco: CA: Jossey-Bass.

Schlechty, P. C. (2005). *Creating great schools: Six critical systems at the heart of educational innovation.* San Francisco: CA: Jossey-Bass.

Spady, W. (1977). Power, authority, and empathy in schooling. In R. A. Carlton, L. A. Colley & N. J. MacKinnon (Eds.), *Education, change and society: A sociology of Canadian education* (pp. 359–375). Toronto, Ontario, Canada: Gage.

For Further Reading

Adler, M. J. (1977). *Reforming education: The opening of the American mind* (2ⁿᵈ ed.). New York, NY: Macmillan.

Berger, P. L. (1963). *Invitation to sociology: A humanistic perspective* (1ˢᵗ ed.). Garden City, NY: Doubleday.

Blank, M. J., Melaville, A., & Shah, B. P. (1999). *Making the difference: Research and practice in community schools.* Washington, DC: Coalition for Community Schools.

Braddock, J. (1990). Tracking the middle grades: National patterns and trends. *Phi Delta Kappan, 71*(6), 445–449.

Caplan, J., Hall, G., Lubin, S., & Fleming, R. (1997). *Literature review of school-family partnerships.* Retrieved February 3, 2007 from http://www.ncrel.org/sdrs/pidata/pi0over.htm

Carter, K. (1993). The place of story in research on teaching and teacher education. *Educational Researcher, 22*(1), 5–12.

Carter, K., & Anders, D. (1996). Program pedagogy. In F. B. Murray (Ed.), *The teacher educator's handbook: Building a knowledge base for the preparation of teachers.* San Francisco: Jossey-Bass.

Carter, K., & Unklesbay, R. (1989). Cases in teaching and law. *Journal of Curriculum Studies, 21,* 527–536.

Clifton, R. A. (1979). Practice teaching: Survival in a marginal situation. *Canadian Journal of Education, 4*(3), 60–74.

Colangelo, N., Assouline, S. G., & Gross, M. (2004). *A nation deceived: How schools hold back America's brightest students.* Iowa City: The Connie Belin & Jacqueline N. Blank International Center for Gifted Education and Talent Development.

Coser, R. L. (1966). Role distance, sociological ambivalence, and transitional status systems. *American Journal of Sociology, 72,* 173–187.

Douvanis, G., & Hulsey, D. (2002). *The least restrictive environment mandate: How has it been defined by the courts?* Retrieved from ERIC database. (ED469442)

Doyle, W. (1986). Themes in teacher education research. In M. C. Wittrock (Ed.), *Handbook of research on teaching* (3rd ed., pp. 3–24). New York: Macmillan.

Doyle, W. (1990). Case methods in the education of teachers. *Teacher Education Quarterly, 17,* 7–15.

Etzioni, A. (1964). *Modern organizations.* Englewood Cliffs, NJ: Prentice-Hall.

Goodlad, J. I. (1990). *Teachers for our nation's schools.* San Francisco: Jossey-Bass.

Greene, M. L., & Campbell, C. (1993). *Becoming a teacher: The contribution of teacher education.* Edmonton, Alberta, Canada: Alberta Education.

Grider, J. (1995). Full inclusion: A practitioner's perspective. *Focus on Autistic Behaviour, 10*(4), 1–12.

Henderson, A., & Berla, N. (Eds.). (1994). *A new generation of evidence: The family is critical to student achievement.* Washington, DC: National Committee for Citizens in Education, Center for Law and Education.

Hollingsworth, S. (1989). Prior beliefs and cognitive change in learning to teach. *American Education Research Journal, 26*(2), 160–189.

Hollowood, T. M., Salisbury, C. l., Rainforth, B., & Palomboro, M. M. (1994). Use of instructional time in classrooms serving students with and without severe disabilities. *Exceptional Children, 61*(3), 242–253.

Ingersoll, R. M. (2007). Short on power, long on responsibility. *Educational Leadership, 65*(1), 20–25.

Kain, D. (1999). Our turn? Teaming and the professional development of teachers. In T. S. Dickinson (Ed.), *Reinventing the middle school* (pp. 201–217). New York: RoutledgeFalmer.

Kardos, S. M., & Morre Johnson, S. (2007). On their own and presumed expert: New teachers' experiences with their colleagues. *Teachers College Record, 109*(9), 2083–2106.

Kindler, A., Badali, S., & Willock, R. (1999). *Between theory and practice: Case studies for learning to teach.* Scarborough, Ontario, Canada: Prentice Hall, Allyn & Bacon Canada.

Leithwood, K., Fullan, M., & Watson, N. (2003). What should be the boundaries of the schools we need? *Education Canada, 43*(1), 12–15.

Lidstone, M., & Hollingsworth, S. (1992). A longitudinal study of cognitive change in beginning teachers: Two patterns of learning to teach. *Teacher Education Quarterly, 19*(4), 39–57.

Lounsbury, J., & Clark, D. (1990). *Inside grade eight: From apathy to excitement.* Reston, VA: National Association of Secondary School Principals.

Loveless, T. (1998). *The tracking and ability grouping debate.* The Thomas Fordham Foundation. Retrieved April 11, 2006, from http://www.edexcellence.net/detail/news.cfm?news_id=127

Manning, M. L., & Bucher, K. (2001). *Teaching in the middle school.* Upper Saddle River, NJ: Merrill Prentice Hall.

McNeill, J. L. (1988). Authority and discipline in schooling. In A. Bomberg (Ed.), *Exploring the teaching milieu* (pp. 61–70). Calgary, Alberta, Canada: Detselig.

Merseth, K. (1991). *The case for cases in teacher education.* Washington, DC: American Association of Colleges for Teacher Education/American Association of Higher Education.

Merseth, K. K., Sommer, J., & Dickstein, S. (2008). Bridging worlds: Changes in personal and professional identities of pre-service urban teachers. *Teacher Education Quarterly 35*(3), 89–108.

Merton, R. K., & Barber, E. (1963). Sociological ambivalence. In E. A. Tiryakian (Ed.), *Sociological theory, values, and sociocultural change: Essays in honor of Pitirim A. Sorokin* (pp. 91–120). London: Free Press of Glencoe.

Noguera, P. A. (2004). Transforming urban schools through investments in the social capital of parents. *In Motion Magazine.* Retrieved April 27, 2005, from http://www.inmotionmagazine.com/er/pn_parents.html.

Schleien, S., & Heyne, L. (1996, May/June). Can I play too? Choosing a community recreation program. *Disability Solutions, 1*(1), 3.

Silberman, C. E. (1971). *Crisis in the classroom: The remaking of American education.* New York, NY: Random House.

Stevenson, C. (2002). *Teaching ten to fourteen year olds.* Boston: Allyn and Bacon.

Taylor, G. T., & Miller, P. J. (1985). Professional course work and the practicum: Do good students make good teachers? *Canadian Journal of Education, 10*(2), 105–120.

Tennent, L., Tayler, C., Farrell, A,.& Patterson, C. (2005). Social capital and sense of community: What do they mean for young children's success at school? International Education Research Conference, Sydney, Australia, Australian Association for Research in Education. Retrieved May 3, 2007, from http://www.aare.edu.au/05pap/ten05115.pdf

Tomlinson, C. A., Tomchin, E. M., Callahan, C. M., Adams, C. M., Pizzat-Tinnin, P., Cunningham, C., et al. (1994). Practices of preservice teachers related to gifted and other academically diverse learners. *Gifted Child Quarterly, 38*(3), 106–114.

Valentine, J. W., Clark, D. C., Hackmann, D. G., & Petzko, V. N. (2002). *A national study of leadership in middle schools. Volume 1: A national study of middle level leaders and school programs.* Reston, VA: National Association of Secondary School Principals.

Vincent, C., Horner, R., & Sugai, G. (2002). Developing social competence for all children. Arlington, VA: ERIC Clearinghouse on Disabilities and Gifted Education (ERIC Document Reproduction Service No. ED468580). Retrieved August 12, 2008, from http://www.eric.ed.gov/ERICDocs/data/ericdocs2sql/content_storage_01/0000019b/80/1a/63/b4.pdf

Wideen, M. F., & Holborn, P. (1986). Research in Canadian teacher education: Promises and problems. *Canadian Journal of Education, 11*(4), 557–583.

Zeichner, K. M., & Gore, J. M. (1990). Teacher socialization. In W. R. Houston, M. Haberman & J. Sikula (Eds.), *Handbook of research in teacher education* (pp. 329–348). New York: Macmillan.

LaVergne, TN USA
17 August 2010
193570LV00002B/1/P